Renegade
Edo and Paris

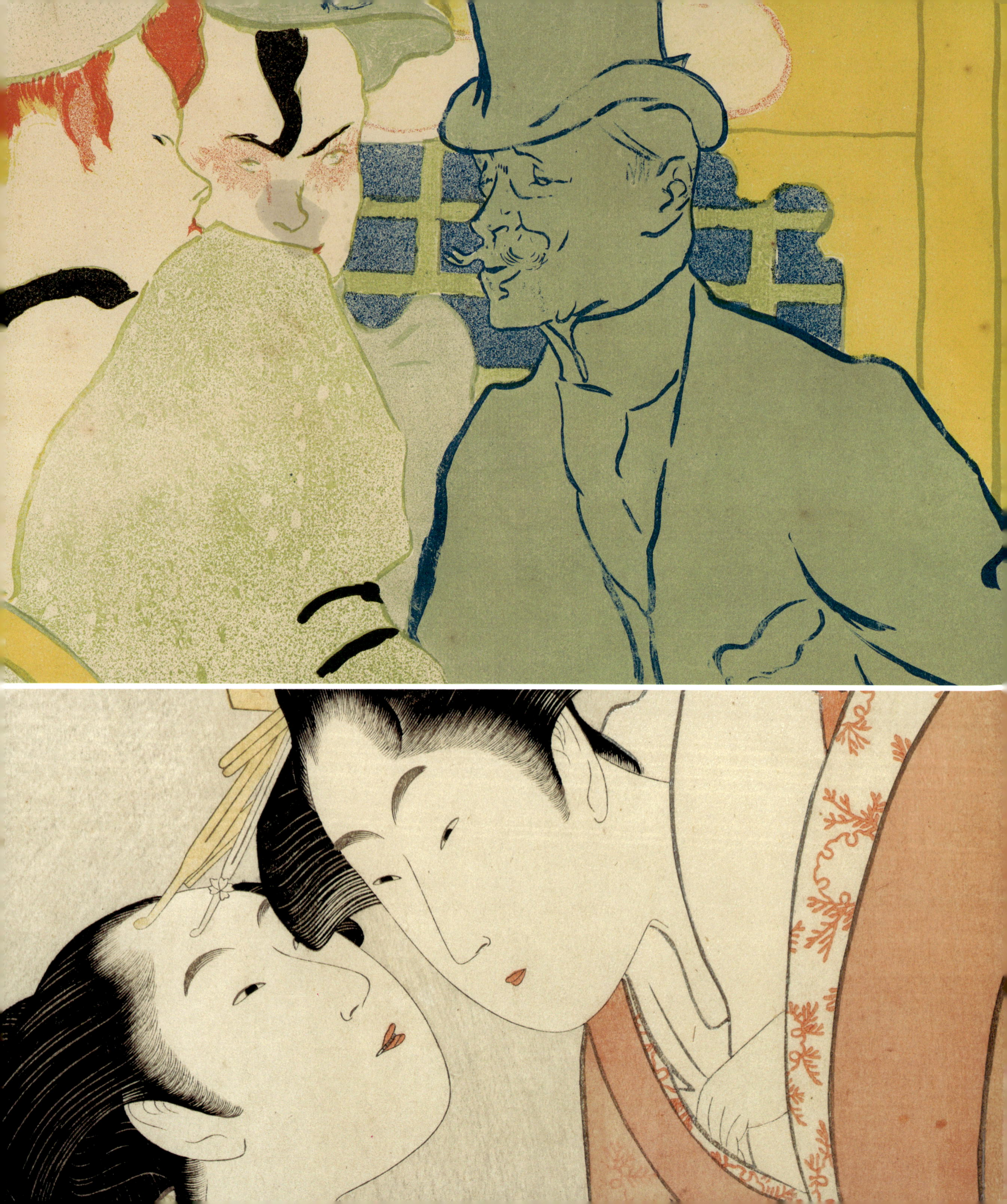

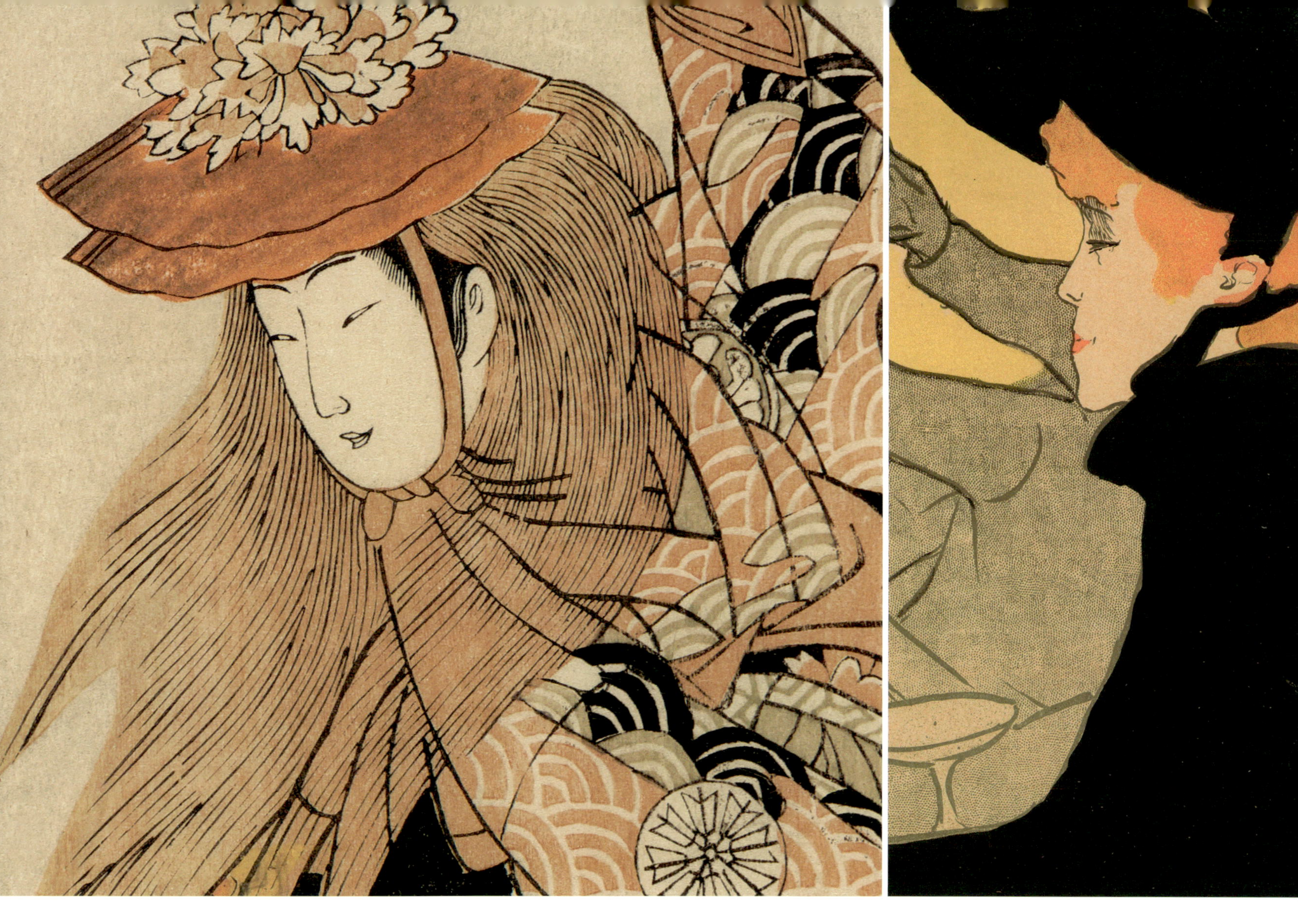

Renegade Edo and Paris

Japanese Prints and Toulouse-Lautrec

Xiaojin Wu

With contributions by
Mary Weaver Chapin

Seattle Art Museum

Contents

Acknowledgments

At the Seattle Art Museum, our collections, exhibitions, and programs showcase art from around the world and build bridges between cultures and centuries. Such is the case with *Renegade Edo and Paris: Japanese Prints and Toulouse-Lautrec*.

Two collectors in Seattle were the inspiration for this exhibition. Allan Kollar, a printmaker and an avid collector of Japanese prints, generously gifted the Seattle Art Museum more than sixty prime examples of Japanese woodblock prints; a few years ago, he introduced us to another Seattle collector, John Price, who has assembled a large holding of Henri de Toulouse-Lautrec's prints over three decades. These works are featured alongside selections from Spencer Hawes, Seattle; Portland Art Museum, Oregon; and Daniel Bergsvik and Donald Hastler, Portland, Oregon. We are also grateful for the generous support of Sebastian Izzard, New York.

Chiyo Ishikawa, our former Susan Brotman Deputy Director for Art and Curator of European Painting and Sculpture, initiated this project. After Ishikawa retired in summer 2020, Xiaojin Wu, our Atsuhiko and Ina Goodwin Tateuchi Foundation Curator of Japanese and Korean Art, reconceptualized the exhibition to focus on the "renegade" aspect of printmaking in both Edo (present-day Tokyo) and Paris. This fresh perspective enables an appreciation of a fascinating body of work beyond its graphic allure. Mary Weaver Chapin, curator of prints and drawings at the Portland Art Museum, has been an indispensable member of this team; her contributions to the exhibition and this catalogue have enhanced our understanding of *japonisme* and the connections between Japanese artists and their French counterparts—chief among them, Toulouse-Lautrec. Thanks are owed to editor Sheri Walter for her attention to detail and expeditious work. We are indebted to Ryan Polich at Marquand Books for the beautiful design of this volume and to Bruno George for his skilled proofreading.

This catalogue was produced through the generous support of Allan and Mary Kollar. The exhibition was made possible through a lead contribution from the Atsuhiko and Ina Goodwin Tateuchi Foundation, generous support from the Katherine Agen Baillargeon Endowment and the Blakemore Foundation, and additional funding from the Mary Ann and Henry James Asian Art Exhibition Endowment. Many individuals at the Seattle Art Museum contributed to this undertaking; their professionalism and dedication to the institution have brought this project to fruition.

Amada Cruz
Illsley Ball Nordstrom Director and Chief Executive Officer
Seattle Art Museum

Introduction

When considering the intriguing parallels in both societal changes and artistic developments in Edo-period (1603–1868) Edo (present-day Tokyo) and late nineteenth-century Paris, it may seem as if history has repeated itself. Both cities were facing challenges to the status quo from the rising middle classes on multiple levels. As an urban culture supported by the new social classes emerged, so did new forms of visual art.

In Edo, townspeople pursued hedonistic lives as a way of defying the state-sanctioned social hierarchy that positioned them at the bottom; their new pastimes supplied subject matter for ukiyo-e (pictures of the floating world). Many such pictures arrived in France in the 1860s, a time when the French art world and society at large were undergoing substantial changes. In Paris, as in Edo, antiestablishment attitudes were on the rise. As artists searched for new and more expressive forms, Henri de Toulouse-Lautrec (1864–1901) and his contemporaries were drawn to novel Japanese prints. While the prints' formal influences—flat forms, cropped compositions, and vibrant colors—on Toulouse-Lautrec and others have been well studied, the shared subversive hedonism that underlies both Japanese prints and Toulouse-Lautrec's work has been less examined.

Through revealing pairings of Japanese and French prints, this exhibition highlights the social impulses—pleasure seeking and theatergoing—behind the burgeoning production of these works in both Edo and Paris, while duly noting stylistic connections. Drawn primarily from a large and important private holding of Toulouse-Lautrec prints and from the Seattle Art Museum's Japanese prints collection, around ninety works offer a critical look at the renegade spirit behind the art's production. "Renegade" captures well the multitude of developments concerning graphic art in both Edo-period Edo and fin-de-siècle Paris: as those cities undertook reforms that generated new thinking on social structure, artists sought novel subjects from popular culture that were not traditionally considered "polite art"; and the mass production and wide distribution of prints promoted appreciation for this medium, eventually elevating it to the level of fine art. It is for these reasons that the exhibition and this catalogue center on this idea of renegade, with the aim of shedding new light on important developments in the history of graphic art—woodblock prints and color lithographs—in each city, to help us better appreciate the works of art and to understand the sociopolitical impetus behind them.

Beyond the seemingly glamourous limelight of "pleasures" were harsh realities, a point that is acknowledged in this catalogue. It also should be noted that the images of dancers, actors, and sex workers are displayed in the gallery for their artistic merit; it is our hope that discussions on the sociopolitical circumstances will help contextualize the artworks' production, so as to not judge them based on today's moral sensibilities. Another important aspect—graphic art's connection with

literature—unfortunately was left out due to the limited scope of this case study, as were both locales' relations with other places beyond the city.

The exhibition is laid out in four sections, and the catalogue echoes that structure. Two essays introduce the floating world of Edo and the bohemian life of Paris, exploring the history of the two cities and the production of ukiyo-e woodblock prints and Toulouse-Lautrec's lithographs. The remaining three sections are organized thematically, each presenting a key aspect of the renegade visual cultures in both cities. "Entertainment" offers a view of Kabuki theaters and teahouses in Edo's Shitamachi (literally, "lower city") and of bohemian nightlife in Parisian dance halls, café-concerts, and theaters. "Celebrity Culture" spotlights the stars of Kabuki theaters and Montmartre cabarets, while "Pleasure Quarters" highlights the women working in licensed brothels and compares the "beautiful women" portrayed in Japanese prints with the unflatteringly candid images of prostitutes in Toulouse-Lautrec's work. We hope this exhibition presents a meaningful comparative study that fosters an appreciation of the distinct yet closely related artistic achievements associated with two different times and places that shared a similar sociopolitical landscape.

Xiaojin Wu

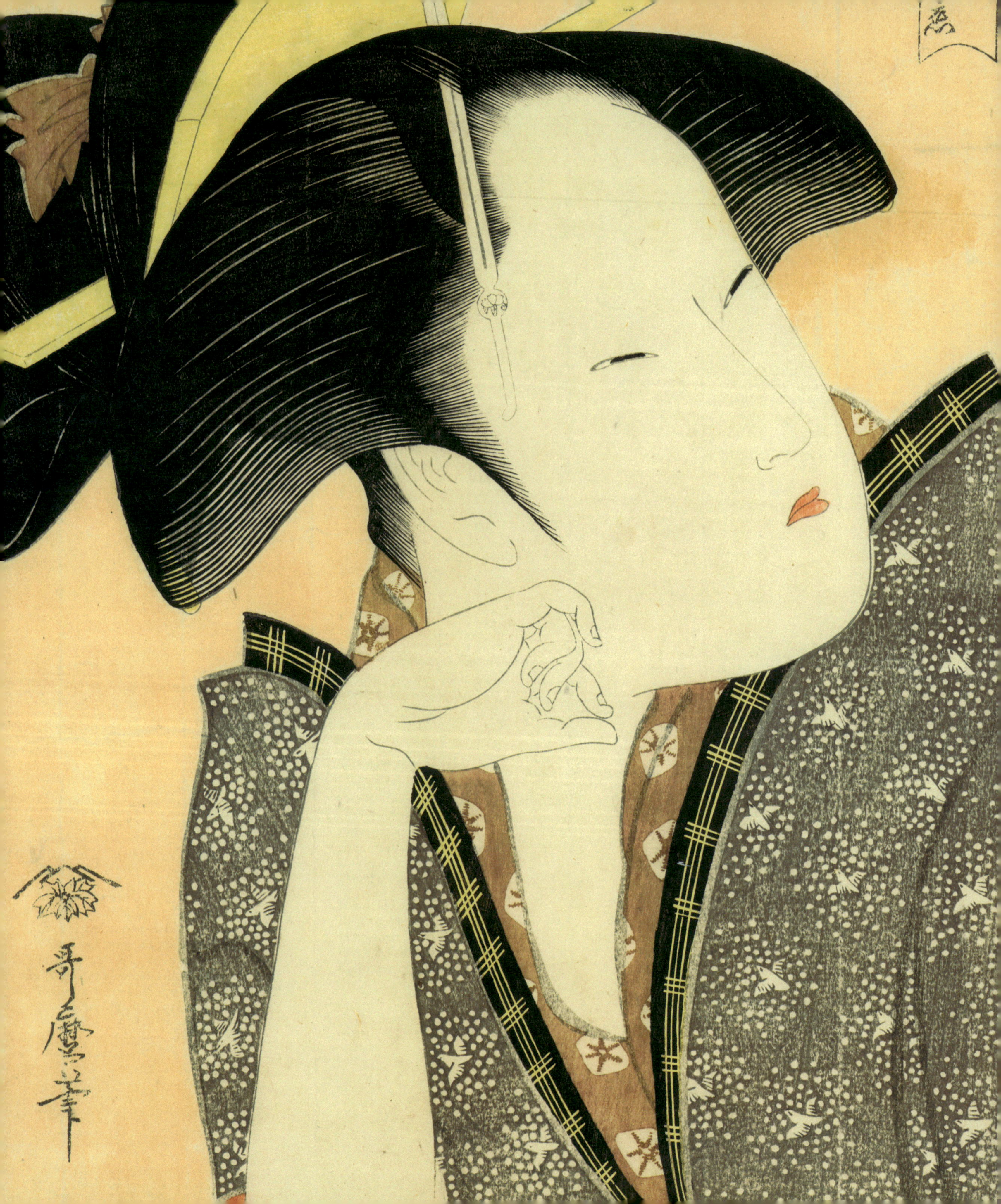

E merging from a century of civil wars, Japan finally saw peace and prosperity along with significant social changes as the Edo period (1603–1868) began. Tokugawa Ieyasu (1543–1616), the first shogun of the last shogunate in Japan, made the city of Edo the capital, instead of the ancient capital Kyoto, where the emperor resided until 1868. That decision had enormous consequences. Resources from all over the country were concentrated in the new capital, and so were consumption and cultural activities. By the eighteenth century, the population of Edo had reached around one million, making it likely the largest city in the world—all the more remarkable because only a century earlier the city was a backwater hundreds of miles away from the metropolises of Kyoto and Osaka. The shogunate created a governing system to ensure an orderly society, but as the city developed—physically, demographically, economically, and culturally—its restrictions ironically led to one unforeseen but major effect: Edo became a magnet for renegades, most notably merchants, performers, and artisans, all of whom contributed to a bustling urban cultural scene that Japan had not seen before. An antiestablishment spirit would come to permeate all aspects of society, from the city itself—given its rivalry with Kyoto—to its townspeople, its urban culture, and the art produced there.

Edo's urban transformation accelerated after 1603 when Ieyasu began his clan's 265-year rule of Japan. The relocation of the shogunal headquarters mobilized manpower for the construction of Edo as the nation's capital, and under the new system of alternate attendance (*sankin kōtai*), which required feudal lords (daimyo) to live in Edo every other year, daimyo arrived with not only their vassals but also their wealth and consumption demands. To provide daily-life services—food, clothing, and lodging—as well as entertainment for the constant incoming stream of samurai, enterprising merchants, artisans, and performers ventured into the city from all over the country, making Edo a hub for innovation and less bound to

Renegade Floating World in Edo

Xiaojin Wu

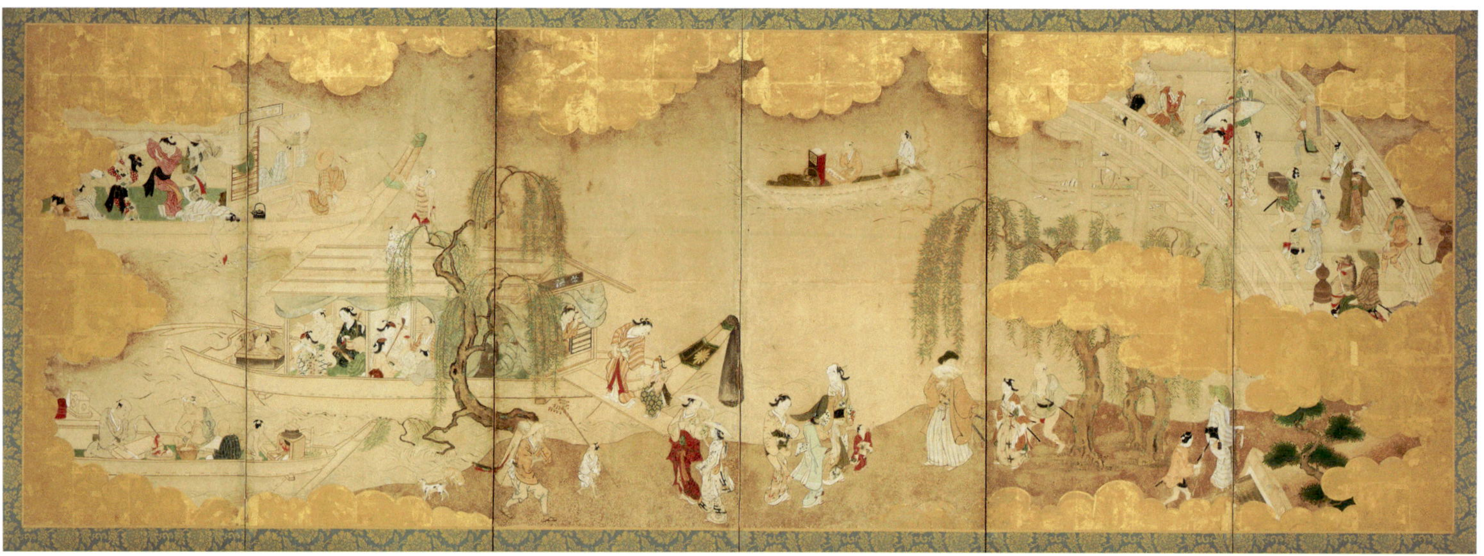

tradition than a more established capital city. To keep pace
with the population growth, the city expanded quickly: more
infrastructure—especially roads—and residences were built,
while commodity trade between Edo and other parts of the
country increased tremendously. By the late seventeenth century,
the once nascent capital city of the shogunate surpassed Kyoto
both in population and in physical area.

The Tokugawa government instituted a rigidly stratified
social order: samurai were at the top, followed by farmers, artisans, and merchants. Each of these groups lived in distinct
parts of Edo. The two bottommost classes lived in the Shitamachi (literally, "lower city") and were often referred to as *chōnin*
(townspeople; literally, "residents of the block"). By the eighteenth century, townspeople constituted about half of the population and congregated in the city to serve the needs of the
large samurai population.[1] Separated from these four classes
and relegated to a status lower even than that of the merchants
were the social outcasts, some of whom were entertainers: they
played an important role, especially in the popularization of
Kabuki theater, and provided services in licensed red-light districts, or the pleasure quarters, a sugar-coated term often used
in this context.

With the increasing economic power of the merchants
and the abundant talents of the artisans, an urban culture soon
bloomed in Edo; it engaged townspeople as well as the samurai class. Of the many pastimes available in the city, the theaters
and the pleasure quarters were the most popular, though visiting
restaurants, teahouses, and seasonal festivals were also among
the regular leisure activities. Writer Asai Ryōi (d. 1691), in his
Tales of the Floating World of about 1665, described the self-
indulgent townspeople as "living only for the moment, savor-
ing the moon, the snow, the cherry blossom, and the maple

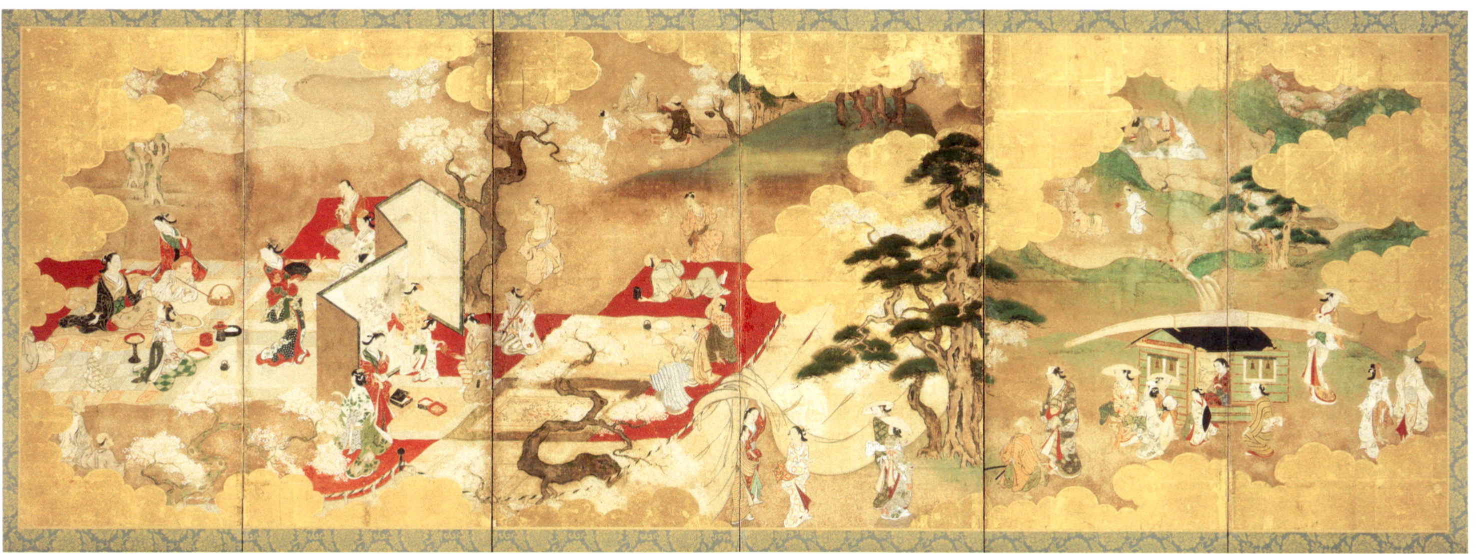

leaves, singing songs, drinking sake, and diverting oneself just
in floating, unconcerned by the prospect of imminent poverty,
buoyant and carefree. . . . [T]his is what we call *ukiyo* (floating
world)."[2] This is thought to be the first appearance of the word
ukiyo, which has the sense of "floating world." The townspeople
were attracted to the lifestyle and aesthetic values of this realm,
which for them was a "strategic response to their exclusion from
political power."[3]

Over the two centuries that followed, the city nurtured a
hedonistic urban subculture, as vividly exemplified in a set of
mid-eighteenth-century screens in the collection of the Seattle
Art Museum [1]. A joyful spring scene unfolds on the right
screen: several groups of people are enjoying music and dance
while eating and drinking under cherry blossoms, as an upper-
class woman arrives in a palanquin with her servants. The
season changes to summer on the left screen, in which Edo residents cool themselves on the Sumida River; on board the boats
are musicians and dancers entertaining the guests, as well as
cooks preparing food. Over the bridge pass people of different
walks of life—samurai on horseback, an itinerant monk, and a
woman with a servant carrying a parasol, among many others.
While keeping in mind that such screens should be considered
judiciously, as they were artistic constructions, not factual doc-
umentation, they can also be viewed as an idealized yet useful
snapshot of daily life in Edo.

Ukiyo-e (pictures of the floating world) encompasses a
variety of artistic output, including brush paintings, privately
commissioned prints, and albums; in a narrow sense, however,
the term refers to woodblock prints produced for popular consumption from the late seventeenth to the late nineteenth century. It is upon this narrow sense of ukiyo-e that this exhibition
catalogue focuses, partly because the sheer number of prints

produced makes them the core of the genre, but also because they offer a meaningful comparative study with the French prints created under Japanese influence.

Individuals were drawn in by the floating world's twin magnets—Kabuki theater and the pleasure quarters—that quickly became the focus of Edo's visual culture, which favored novel themes and bold forms in contrast with the more traditional, conservative, and elite tastes of Kyoto. It is conventionally thought that Kabuki theater originated in comic dances performed in the early seventeenth century by a troupe of women on a bank of Kyoto's Kamo River. But there is little doubt that Kabuki gained its broad appeal in Edo. There, a "rough stuff" (*aragoto*) style of acting was developed by famed actor Ichikawa Danjūrō I (1660–1704), in contrast with the soft (*wagoto*) style favored in Kyoto and Osaka. Danjūrō's exaggerated and dynamic expressions on the stage were quickly transferred to graphic forms in prints, such as those by Torii Kiyonobu I (1644–1729). Generations of actors of the Ichikawa line and artists of the Torii lineage have carried on these artistic practices to the present. Torii Kiyonobu II's (1706–1763) print of Ebizō II (formerly Danjūrō II) (1688–1758) performing in *Shibaraku* (Wait a Minute!) is one telling example of the legacy of both the subject and the artist (fig. 1). Prints of Kabuki actors onstage and behind the scenes were hugely popular among Kabuki fans; they became one of the key subgenres of ukiyo-e.

The licensed brothel district called Yoshiwara was established in 1617 near Nihonbashi in the center of the city; it moved to the northern outskirts after the devastating fire in 1657 and was renamed Shin (New) Yoshiwara. The women employed in Yoshiwara were assigned ranks.[4] A geisha (literally, "a person with artistic skills") was usually trained in music and dance. Geisha worked as entertainers but often also engaged in prostitution, despite the prohibition on this practice introduced in the mid-eighteenth century. *Yūjo* (literally, "play woman") were primarily sex workers in the licensed district.[5] Most frequently featured in prints are the high-ranking *yūjo*, for they were the most desirable not only for their beauty but also for their skills in music, dance, calligraphy, and even poetry, as they would be expected to exchange love letters or poems with their clients. Although Kabuki actors and beautiful women in pleasure quarters became the primary subjects of commercially successful prints, they were still treated as social outcasts by the government. The prints associated with them represented an alternative to the official culture supported by the shogunate or the court culture endorsed by the emperor and were therefore often censored.

Until the mid-seventeenth century, most publications relating to or distributed in Edo were printed in Kyoto. The first guidebook to the city, *Edo meishoki* (Record of Famous Places in Edo), was published in Kyoto in 1662. With the growing demand for books in Edo, publishing began to flourish

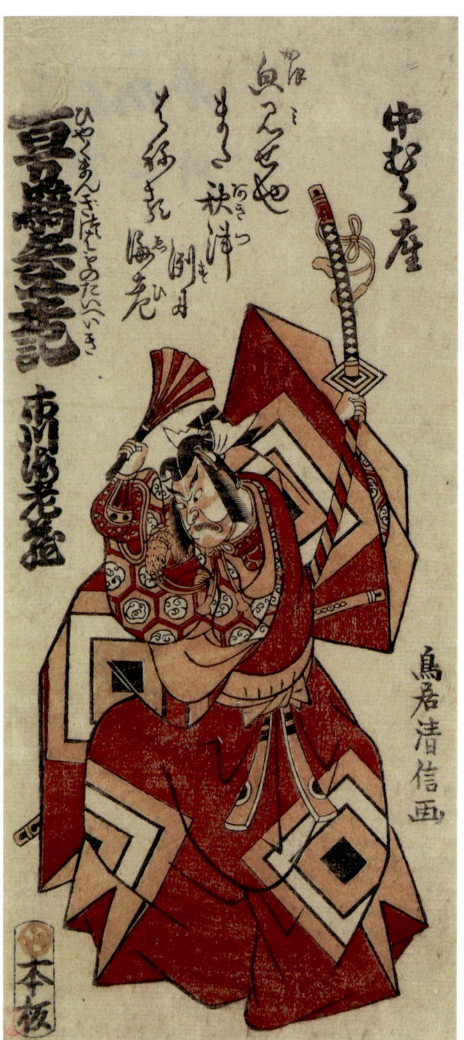

FIG. 1
Torii Kiyonobu II, *Actor Ichikawa Ebizō in Shibaraku*, 1753, woodblock print in "*hosoban*" format, Harvard Art Museums / Arthur M. Sackler Museum, Gift of the Friends of Arthur B. Duel, 1933.4.1560

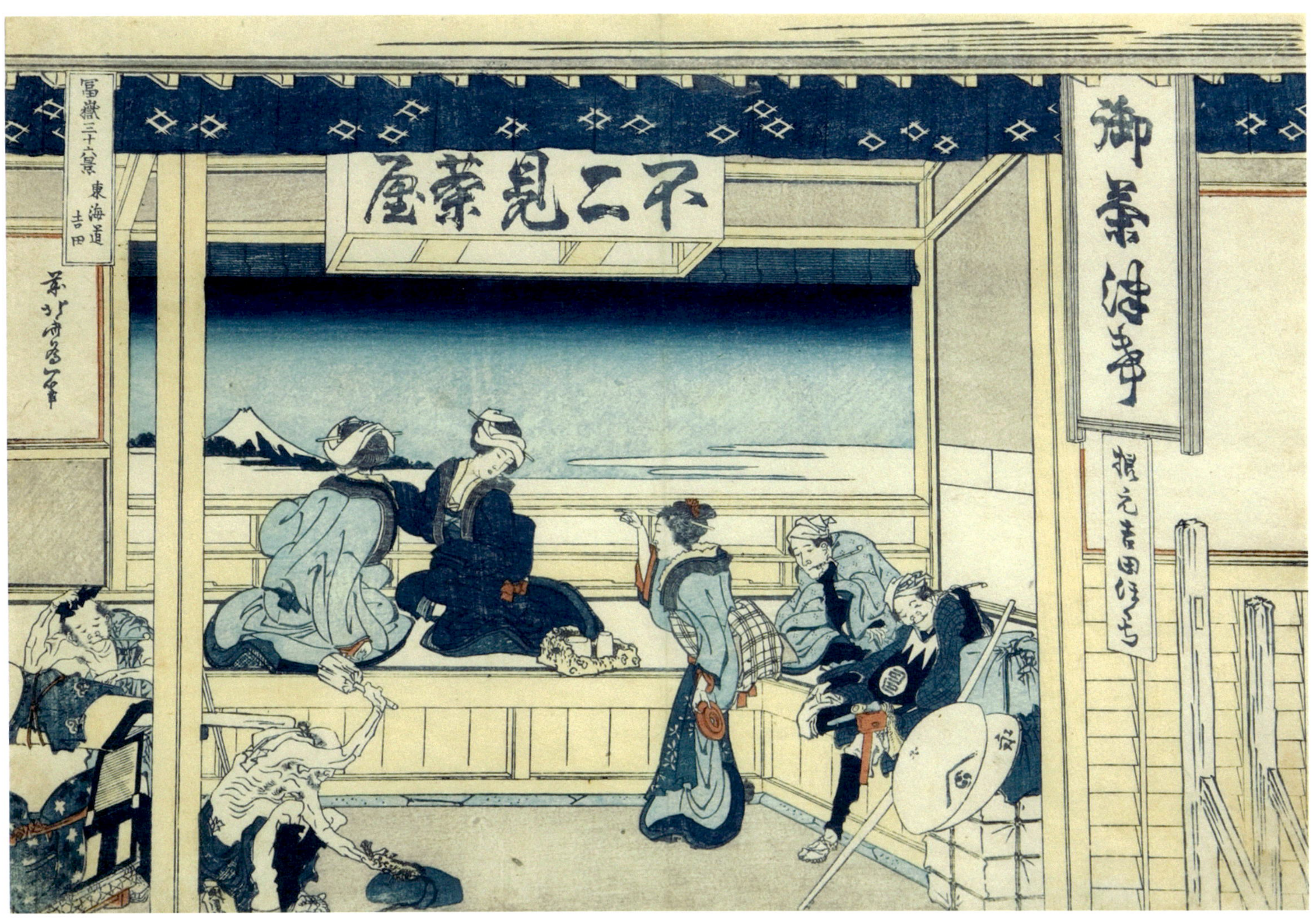

PLATE 2

Katsushika Hokusai, *Yoshida on the Tōkaidō*, from the series *Thirty-Six Views of Mount Fuji*, ca. 1830–32, woodblock print

The first major landscape series in the history of Japanese prints is Katsushika Hokusai's *Thirty-Six Views of Mount Fuji*, which includes the famed *Great Wave*. This print focuses on people at a teahouse more than on the mountain itself, with a view of Fuji in the distance on the left. The series was instantly popular after its launch in the New Year of 1831, so the publisher expanded it by ten designs. **XW**

there in the mid- to late seventeenth century, and by the 1760s, Edo had become the epicenter of printing culture. Commercial prints served as advertisements for Kabuki theaters, pleasure quarters, restaurants, and tourist sites, while privately commissioned works were produced for poetry clubs. The medium—woodblock printing—allowed a vast output, making prints both affordable for mass consumption and a channel for artists to exercise their creativity. However, the prints were not made by the artist alone; it was a collaborative process involving an "ukiyo-e quartet"—the publisher, artist, block carver, and printer.[6] As a kind of ubiquitous commodity, prints were widely collected by the newly rich urbanites—the merchant class, as well as samurai.

As discussed in Mary Weaver Chapin's essay in this catalogue, a large influx of Japanese printed materials began to arrive in Europe in the mid-nineteenth century, climaxing with the *Exposition des maîtres Japonais* in 1890 at the École des

Beaux-Arts, which included more than one thousand wood-block prints, illustrated books, and painted hanging scrolls. French artists' encounter with Japanese prints was a timely one: in search of new paths to social and artistic revolution, they found them in the novel ukiyo-e prints coming from afar.[7] While the graphic language—bold lines, flat forms, and cropped compositions—and subject matter of ukiyo-e prints clearly impacted French prints, the woodcut medium was not widely deployed. Most late nineteenth-century French artists— including Henri de Toulouse-Lautrec (1864–1901)—opted for lithography for their work. Henri Rivière's (1864–1951) *Breton Landscapes*, produced in the 1890s, is one of a few exceptional examples of woodcut printing. Even Rivière turned to lithography for his *Thirty-Six Views of the Eiffel Tower* [4], a direct homage to Katsushika Hokusai's (1760–1849) *Thirty-Six Views of Mount Fuji* [2]: each depicts an iconic landmark in different seasons, at various times of the day, and from multiple vantage points. Ironically, by the 1860s, when French artists were introduced to ukiyo-e prints, Edo was already transitioning into Tokyo, the modern capital of Japan. The floating world Toulouse-Lautrec and his contemporaries saw through eighteenth- and early nineteenth-century Japanese prints was in a sense a fantasy—the disappearing city of Edo.

NOTES

1. See Katō Takashi, "Edo in the Seventeenth Century: Aspects of Urban Development in a Segregated Society," *Urban History* 27, no. 2 (August 2000): 189–210.

2. Hickman, "Views of the Floating World," 6.

3. Guth, *Art of Edo Japan*, 30.

4. For a detailed account of women working in Yoshiwara, see Asano Shūgō, "Courtesans, Geisha, and Male Prostitutes," in Morse, *Drama and Desire*, 41–49.

5. Julie Nelson Davis, in her most recent publication, *Picturing the Floating World*, makes a convincing argument about the English terminology that best describes the women working in Yoshiwara, 36–37.

6. Davis, *Partners in Print*, 191.

7. Ives, *The Great Wave*, 21.

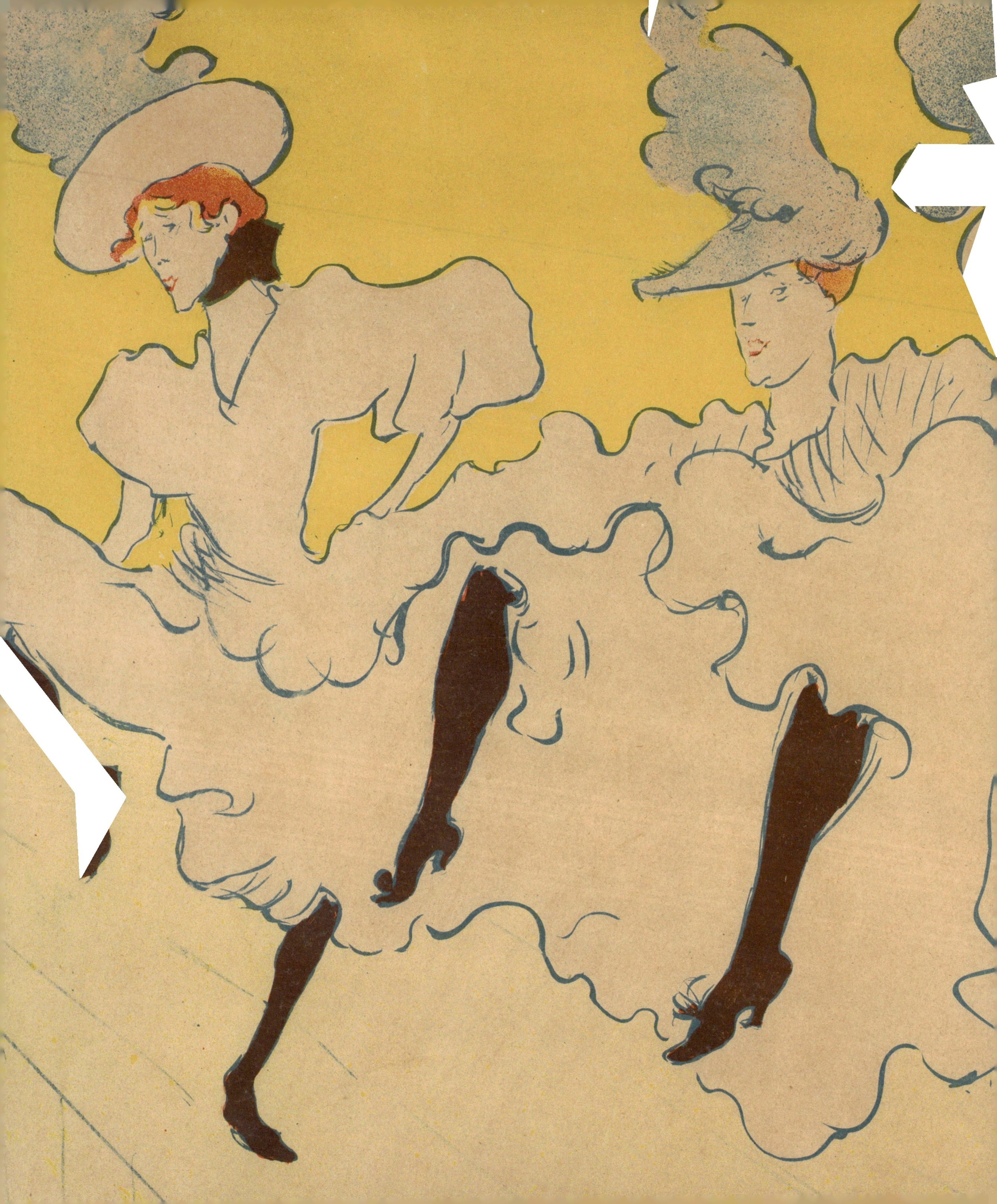

By the time artist Henri de Toulouse-Lautrec (1864–1901) moved to Paris in 1882 from his home in Southern France, the metropolis boasted an international reputation as the City of Light. The establishment of the Third Republic in 1871 had ushered in an era of stability and prosperity, one that allowed for the flourishing of art, science, and technology. Paris's reputation was not only wide, but varied: for some, it was the center of industrial progress, where mighty locomotives billowed steam across the cityscape, and where, in 1889, Gustave Eiffel would build his famous iron-framed tower soaring one thousand feet into the Parisian sky. For others, Paris was the intellectual capital, the home of eighteenth-century philosophers who had ushered in the Enlightenment as well as the contemporary writers and poets exploring Naturalism, Symbolism, and Decadence. Others looked to Paris as the epicenter of fashion, style, and gastronomy. Perhaps above all else, Paris was considered the European center of entertainment, boasting everything from the most elite operas, theaters, and ballets to working-class dance halls, popular circuses, and artistic cabarets. These attributes, and the mythology that surrounded them, would later prompt writer and philosopher Walter Benjamin to proclaim Paris the capital of the nineteenth century.[1]

This was the heady world that Toulouse-Lautrec entered when he came to Paris to pursue an artistic career. As the only surviving son of an old aristocratic family, he made the unusual choice to pursue a paid profession (rather than the idle leisure typical of his class), hinting at the contrarian tendencies that would mark his life and art. He initially attended the atelier of Fernand Cormon, and then joined the spirited group of students at the Académie Julian. There, he was surrounded by like-minded individuals who also craved freedom from artistic formulae and the deadening conformity of bourgeois life under the Third Republic. Toulouse-Lautrec immersed himself in this "Bohemia," a term that first emerged earlier in the nineteenth

Bohemian Paris and the Prints of Toulouse-Lautrec

Mary Weaver Chapin

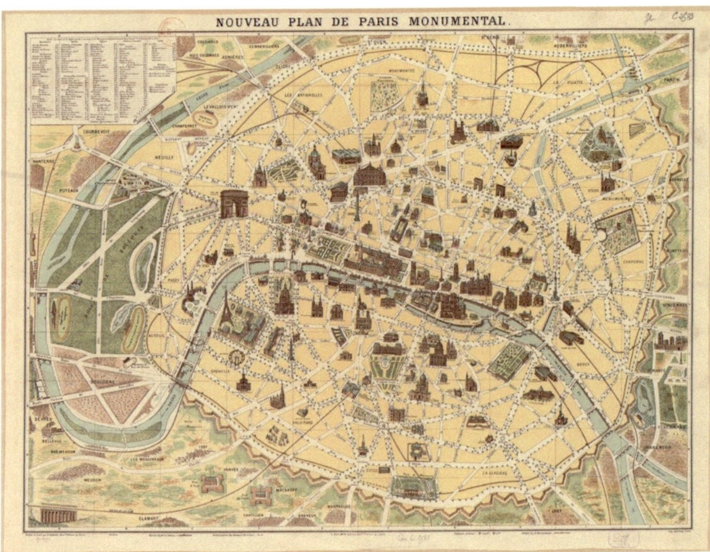

century to describe young artists, writers, drifters, and dreamers on the margins of society.[2] Rather than a specific locale, Bohemia was a state of mind, a subculture, and an attitude toward living. Nor was Bohemia a monolithic culture: there were many "bohemias," even within a single city. For Toulouse-Lautrec and his fellow painters, however, Bohemia meant an appetite for novelty and adventure mixed with a willful disregard for tradition and rules. In this sense, it is analogous to the "renegade" Edo described by Xiaojin Wu in this volume—an ersatz Parisian "floating world."

In Toulouse-Lautrec's day, the center of bohemian Paris was Montmartre, a neighborhood on the northern edge of the city (fig. 2). Then still dotted with windmills and small farms, Montmartre had once been a separate community clustered on the steep hillside of the butte more than four hundred feet above the city. The neighborhood had long held a reputation as a frontier district, poised between country and city, lawlessness and order, invention and conformity. It was a haven for outsiders, artists, and students who were drawn to the inexpensive rent and the cheap entertainment. A spirit of rebellion— by turns gently humorous or deeply scathing—characterized this quartier and its inhabitants. The approaching fin de siècle seemed to portend a collapse of established norms, and the term itself became synonymous with a sense of world-weariness. To escape (or indulge?) this nihilism, artists, including Toulouse-Lautrec, self-medicated with the hallucinogenic and powerful spirit absinthe and flung themselves into the array of bohemian entertainments of Montmartre.

Chief among them was the *cabaret-artistique* the Chat Noir, which opened in 1881 at the foot of the butte. Owner and impresario Rodolphe Salis kept patrons entertained with cheap beer, poetry readings, a rotating art gallery, and performances by

L. Guilmin, *Nouveau Plan de Paris Monumental*, 1899, Source gallica.bnf.fr / Bibliothèque nationale de France

rising stars of the entertainment industry, including Aristide Bruant, whom Toulouse-Lautrec would so memorably portray in his prints. Significantly, the Chat Noir was also the home of a highly inventive *theatre d'ombres* (shadow theater). Shadow theaters are common in many cultures, including Japan, and the Chat Noir's productions helped fuel the vogue for *japonisme* as well as the inventive use of shadows in pictorial art. The Moulin Rouge opened in Montmartre in 1889, adding to the lure of the neighborhood. At this notorious dance hall, professional dancers performed the scandalous cancan while working-class artists, models, and laborers rubbed shoulders with aristocrats "slumming" in the district. Just steps away, thrill seekers could visit the Cirque Fernando, the elegant Divan Japonais café-concert, and Bruant's cabaret, or stroll south to the Folies Bergère to see the mesmerizing veil dances of Loïe Fuller, or laugh at the double entendres of diseuse Yvette Guilbert at La Scala. In other words, the volume and variety of amusements far exceeded the capacity for any one person to sample them all.

To advertise these and other entertainments, promoters relied on the relatively new medium of lithography. Starting in the late 1860s, artist Jules Chéret (1836–1932) brought a new artistic sensibility, a creative use of color, and an entrepreneurial genius to the production of the poster. Chéret's designs advertised the burgeoning entertainments and commodities of Paris and created an open-air museum of playful characters. Paris became a city of posters: they were found on billboards, kiosks, public urinals, shop windows, omnibuses, and Morris columns, whose sole function was to display theater posters. This explosion surrounded pedestrians with attractive lures to endless entertainment, further enhancing the myth of Paris as a playground. Their sheer ubiquity altered the visual experience of the city; by one estimate, more than 1.5 million designs appeared annually in Paris by the end of the century.[3]

Not only did Chéret's posters advertise the ever-changing world of pleasures to be found in Paris, they also played a role in the development of the *estampe originale* (original print) movement. For centuries, fine prints were associated with traditional techniques such as woodcut, engraving, and etching. The invention of lithography by Alois Senefelder in the 1790s was the first significant addition to the printmaking media in centuries. Its initial practical use was as a method of reproducing sheet music in large quantities, a fact that linked it intimately to commercial production. Artists, especially in England and France, experimented with lithography early in the nineteenth century, yielding beautiful results that captured the autographic qualities of drawing on stone. Chéret's forays into color lithography for advertising posters brought a new level of artistic innovation. Though lithography was still tied to commerce, artists began to see the potential of this medium for new ends.

By the 1890s, color lithography was the most exciting new tool for European artists, who recognized the opportunity to

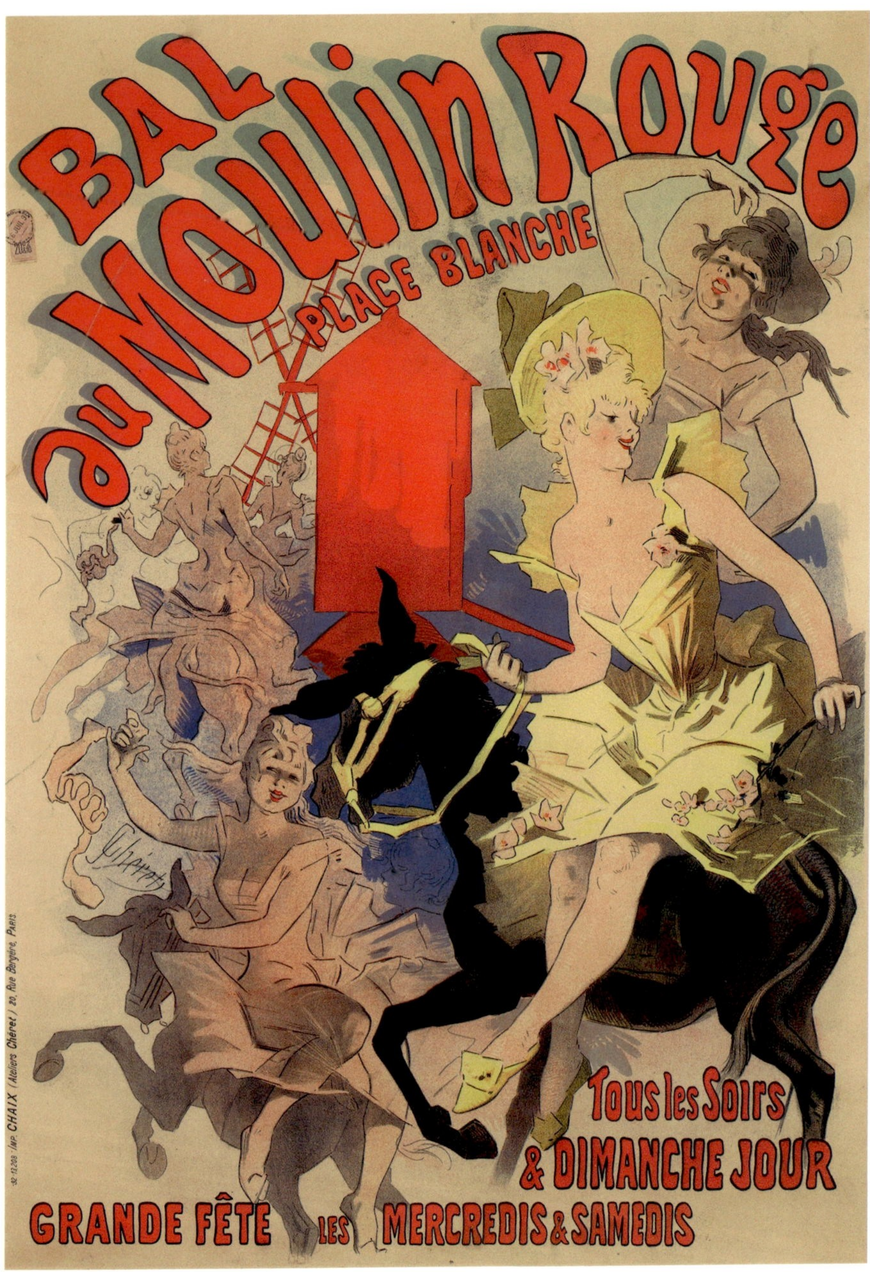

innovate. Its taint as a commercial medium may have held some appeal as well: it freed artists from the baggage and history that accompanied centuries-old techniques such as woodcut and intaglio, and it carried a whiff of transgression, a scent attractive to these avant-garde artists. Not only was the medium considered suspect, but so, too, was the use of color. For generations, treasured prints—works by Old Masters such as Albrecht Dürer and Rembrandt van Rijn—featured black ink on white paper. While hand-colored impressions were occasionally produced, color was antithetical to the concept of a fine print. Yet with

PLATE 3
Jules Chéret, *Ball at the Moulin Rouge*, 1889, color lithograph

Known as the "father of the poster," Jules Chéret produced advertisements that created a plein-air museum of colorful designs touting the pleasures of Paris. This iconic poster trumpeted the opening of the famous dance hall where Henri de Toulouse-Lautrec and so many of the celebrities he depicted would make their names. **MWC**

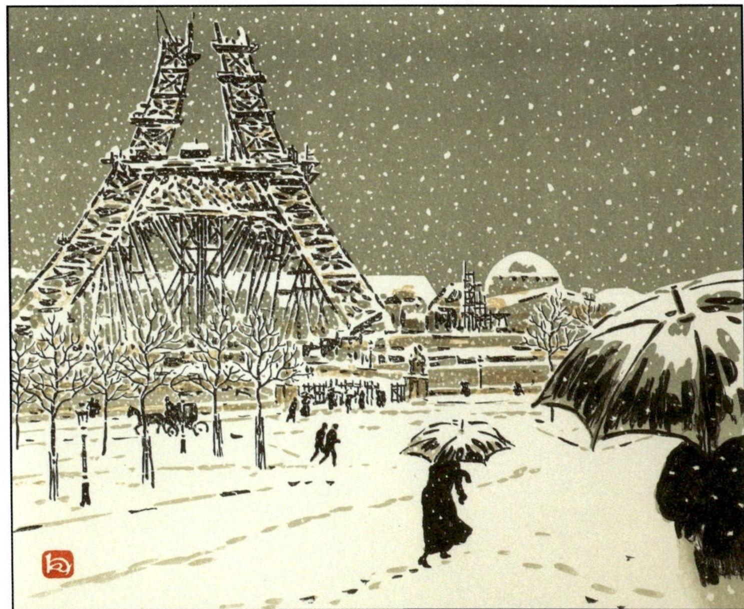

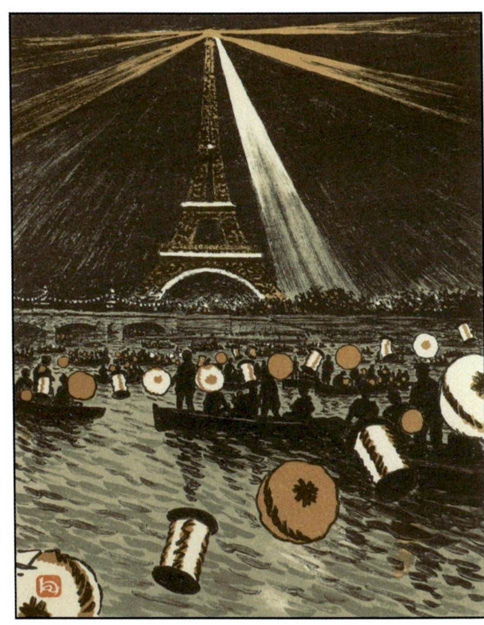

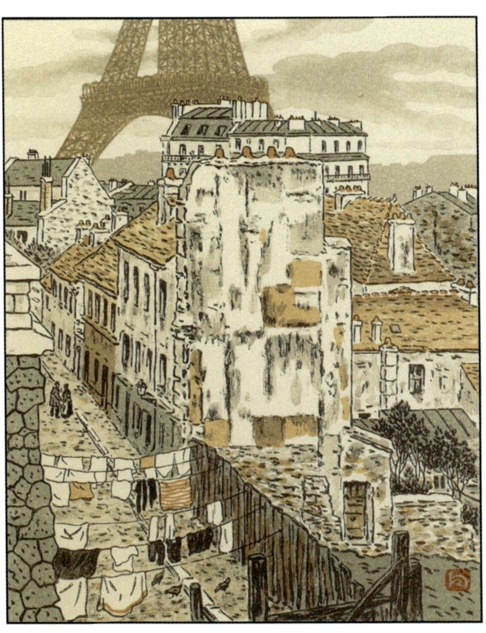

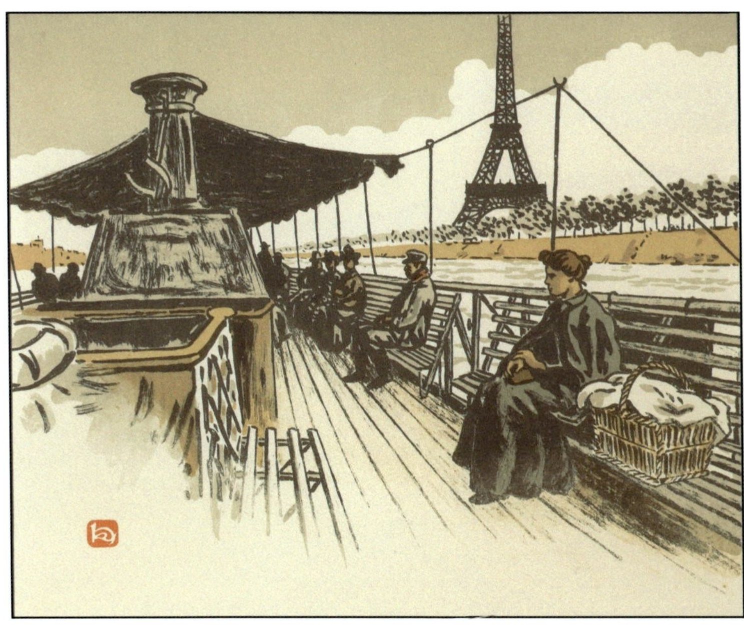

PLATE 4
Henri Rivière, *Thirty-Six Views of the Eiffel Tower*,
1902, album of 36 color lithographs

Inspired by Katsushika Hokusai's images of
Mount Fuji, Henri Rivière depicted the construction of the Eiffel Tower through various
vantage points, seasons, and moods. He incorpo-
rated details of the daily lives of Parisians as well,
including the workers, neighbors, and passersby
who stopped to marvel at the growing monument.
MWC

the advent of lithography, and advances in printing, the 1890s
became known as the "color revolution," in which printmakers
employed vibrant, garish, and experimental hues, often up to
a dozen in a single print; techniques such as rainbow rolls and
spatter; and metallic pigments to enhance their designs. Artists
and the public delighted in these creations, even if the establishment did not: they were forbidden in the official art exhibitions
of Paris (the Salon) until 1899, and critics railed against the taint
of commerce they associated with lithography and the colors
that they considered too garish for fine art. It is no wonder that

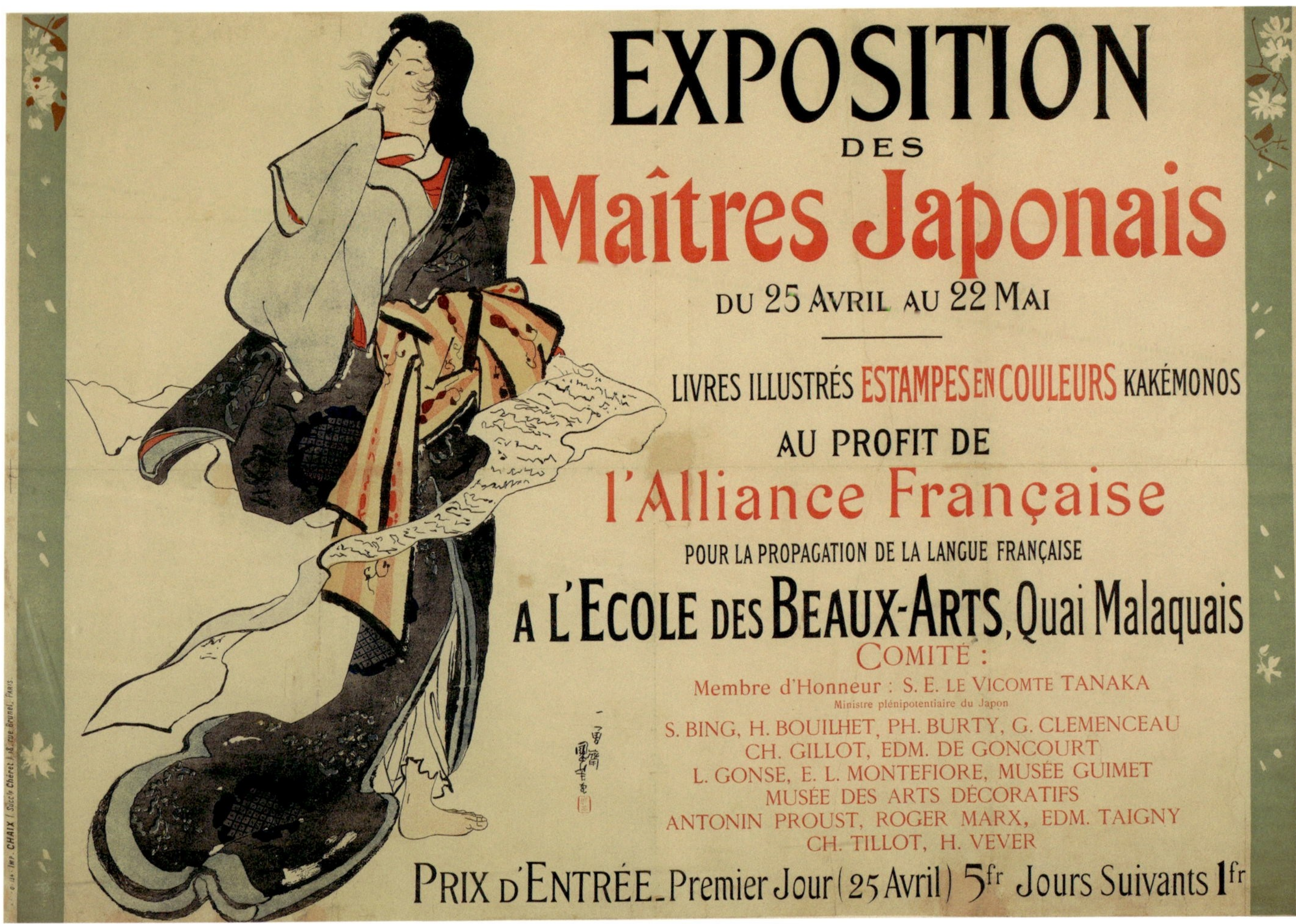

renegade artists such as Toulouse-Lautrec took this as their invitation to thumb their noses at the establishment and commit ever more seriously to the color print.

Renegade Edo and Paris aims to shed new light on *japonisme* by exploring the social impulses that connected the two cities, while also calling attention to the thematic and stylistic similarities between French artists and their Japanese counterparts.[4] The first wave of Japanese material—including prints, illustrated books, hanging scrolls, and textiles—entered France in the mid-century. By the early 1860s, Japanese products were available for purchase in Parisian department stores, prompting a rage for all things Japanese. In 1872, critic Philippe Burty coined the term *japonisme* to capture this growing passion, which was further accelerated by the success of the Japanese participation at the World's Fairs in Paris in 1867, 1878, 1889, and 1900. The first artists to incorporate Japanese elements into their paintings tended to use them as props: scrolls or screens were included as decoration in the backgrounds of Impressionist paintings and elegant kimonos and fans were donned by their models.

PLATE 5
Jules Chéret, *Exhibition of Japanese Prints*, 1890, color lithograph

To suggest the content of this sprawling exhibition, Jules Chéret used the figure of a *yūjo* (sex worker; literally, "play woman") holding a letter and stripes of green on either edge to imitate the mounting silks used in traditional Japanese hanging scrolls. Unlike Henri de Toulouse-Lautrec, who would absorb and transmute Eastern compositional idioms, Chéret was content to borrow motifs directly from the source. **MWC**

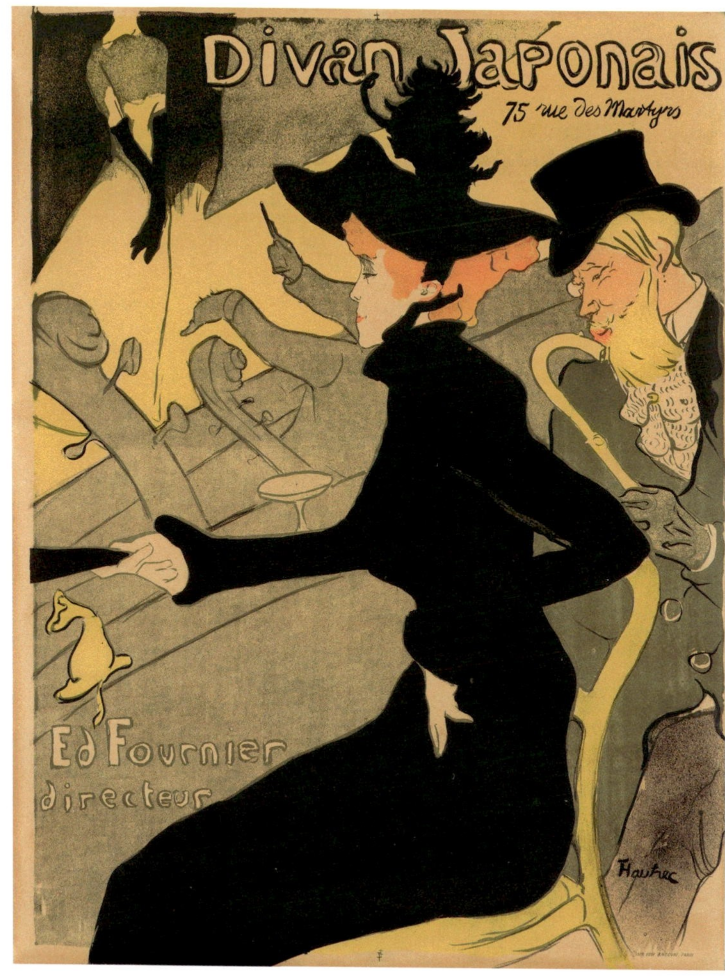

PLATE 6
Henri de Toulouse-Lautrec, *Divan Japonais*, 1892,
color lithograph

Capitalizing on the rage for all things Japanesque, this café-concert offered the latest in
French entertainment in a pseudo-Japanese inte-
rior. Here, the artist depicts dance star Jane Avril
in an elegant profile enjoying a performance of
Yvette Guilbert. **MWC**

The next generation of French artists advanced the use
of Japanesque idioms, adopting asymmetrical arrangements,
cropped views, and the use of flattened color and perspective
that they admired in ukiyo-e prints. When, in 1890, the École
des Beaux-Arts launched the influential *Exposition des maîtres
Japonais* [5], featuring more than one thousand objects, French
artists could immerse themselves in the material as never before.
Among his contemporaries, Toulouse-Lautrec stood out for his
creative assimilation of these techniques, which he pushed to
his own unique ends. Elements of Japanese inspiration can be
found throughout his oeuvre, as illustrated in this catalogue,
from the silhouetted form of Aristide Bruant [35] to the flow-
ing, calligraphic line of cancan dancers' skirts [13, 30, 33] to his
stylized monograph—"HT-L" inscribed in a circle—that he
designed in imitation of Japanese artist and censor seals.

Yet beyond these stylistic echoes, Toulouse-Lautrec found
validation for his own work in the motifs of the prostitutes,
nightlife, and celebrities of ukiyo-e prints. Moreover, he shared
an interest in the "renegades" who featured in the Japanese

woodblocks. As in Edo, performers, despite their wide popular appeal, were still considered to be outside polite society. As such, they were liminal characters, entertaining mixed-class audiences but rising from the lowest ranks. Many of the French performers were highly attuned to this paradox as they honed their reputation as daring outsider artists while playing to the bourgeoisie, and, in fact, growing richer themselves. A case in point was the chansonnier Bruant, who capitalized on his gruff style while eventually earning enough to retire to the countryside to his own chateau. Others, however, like the cancan dancer La Goulue, were less fortunate. Her star shone brightly for a short time as she became the talk of *tout Paris*, but it soon faded, and she died in poverty. These trajectories were played out in Japan as well. Thus, we see even further parallels between Bruant and the dashing actors who entertained Edo and between famous performers such as Jane Avril and Loïe Fuller and the "beautiful women" found in ukiyo-e prints. In this way, the resonances between Edo and Paris constitute a web of connections formed by the shared strands of social daring, formal innovation, and exquisite printmaking.

NOTES

1. See Benjamin, "Paris, the Capital of the Nineteenth Century," in *Walter Benjamin: Selected Writings*, vol. 3, *1935–1938*, ed. Howard Eiland and Michael W. Jennings, trans. Edmund Jephcott et al. (Cambridge, MA: Belknap, 2002), 32–49.

2. The term "Bohemia" was first used in this way around 1830 and was widely popularized by Henri Murger's 1851 novel *Scènes de la vie de bohème*, followed by Giacomo Puccini's 1896 opera *La Bohème*. For a full account of the concept of Bohemia in its many iterations in the fine arts, see Sylvain Amic, *Bohèmes: de Léonard de Vinci à Picasso*, exh. cat. (Paris: Réunion des Musées Nationaux, 2012).

3. D'Avenel, *Le Mécanisme de la vie moderne*, 162.

4. The literature on the stylistic borrowings of French artists from Japanese sources is vast. For an excellent general introduction from 1974, see Ives, *The Great Wave*. For more recent considerations, see Breuer, *Japanesque* (2010), and Burnham, Thompson, and Braun, *Looking East* (2014).

Catalogue Entries

Entertainment
Shitamachi and Montmartre

The city of Edo can broadly be divided into two spheres: Shitamachi (literally, "lower city"), the mercantile district near the bay, to which townspeople were legally restricted; and Yamanote, the hilly residential area reserved for lords and retainers (fig. 3). This division was as much social and cultural as geographic. The hedonistic atmosphere in Shitamachi was in stark contrast to the stoic, restrained, rigidly defined social life of Yamanote. The distinctive subculture of the lower city was best represented in its popular entertainment: sumo wrestling, Kabuki theater, and music and dance in the teahouses and the pleasure quarters. Shitamachi, home to many artists, was also a locale for a range of nonconforming social activities.

Likewise, Montmartre, Paris's fin-de-siècle entertainment district, was not only a physical location but a social environment; it had its own class structure, economy, and subculture, as Mary Weaver Chapin notes in her essay, and served as the gathering place for bohemians. Reversing the topography of Edo, in Paris, the entertainment district was found on hilly Montmartre, while the more respectable recreations were located on the flat plain below. In Pierre Vidal's 1897 design for *La Vie à Montmartre*, a group of Montmartre inhabitants—cancan dancer, artist,

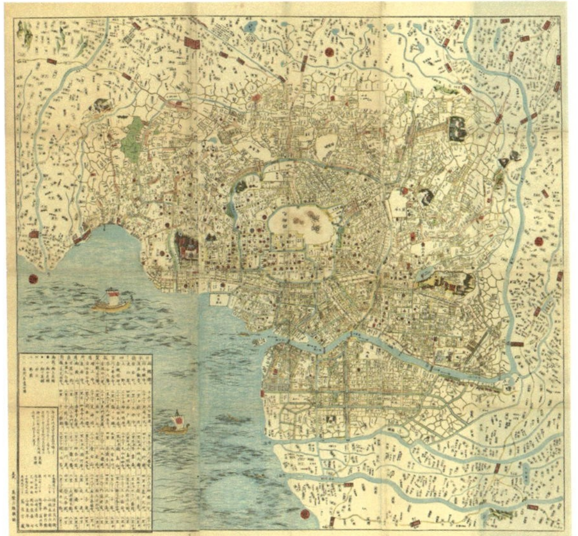

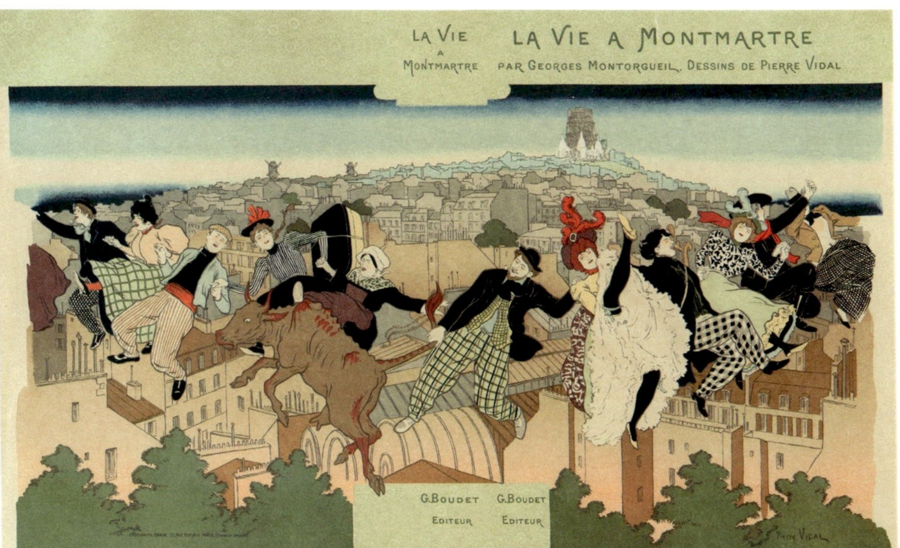

streetwalker, and pimp—float in midair against the backdrop of the hillscape (fig. 4). The sky in the distance is depicted in graduated blue bands, a graphic feature often seen in Japanese landscape prints by artists such as Katsushika Hokusai (1760–1849) and Utagawa Hiroshige (1797–1858). Montmartre was also a place where antiestablishment attitudes could be expressed, and a place that signified the unusual or unconventional.

Perhaps most pertinent to this exhibition is the shared nature of Shitamachi and Montmartre as entertainment hubs and gathering places for artists, writers, musicians, and performers. Both Japanese and French prints capture the vibrant energy of these districts' social venues. In Shitamachi, one of the most popular activities was Kabuki theater. Flamboyant actors, the onstage heroes, became sensations both in the theater and in prints. In countless images, artists creatively depicted actors' exaggerated expressions and striking poses with daring compositions [7]. Entertainment in teahouses [11, 12] and beautiful, idealized waitresses [10] were also common subjects.

Montmartre—its dance halls and café-concerts in particular—was the center of Henri de Toulouse-Lautrec's (1864–1901) social life and career. It was in Montmartre that he encountered dancers, singers, and prostitutes who would become the subject of his work, and through his representations of those on the fringes of society, he crafted his own version of modern life. His iconic poster *Moulin Rouge: La Goulue* [13], for example, positioned the famous cancan dancer La Goulue against the silhouette of a crowd. The use of shadow was informed by the shadow plays at the Chat Noir cabaret [14] developed by Henri Rivière (1864–1951) and others from Japanese prototypes. The flat silhouettes and subtle colors of shadow plays resonated with the modernist concerns of Toulouse-Lautrec and his contemporaries.[1] Japanese artists such as those of the Utagawa school had effectively employed the shadow decades earlier to add suggestive touches in their prints [11, 12]. Formal features frequently found in Japanese prints—figures in profile view, pronounced contour lines, and flat shapes—became idioms in Toulouse-Lautrec's graphic language. During the mid-1890s, he gradually shifted his interest toward more highbrow theaters, opera, and concert halls, as the theater programs [17] and playbills he designed demonstrate. **XW**

NOTE

1. Cate, "The Social Menagerie of Toulouse-Lautrec's Montmartre," in Thomson, Cate, and Chapin, *Toulouse-Lautrec and Montmartre*, 38.

PLATE 7
Utagawa Kunisada, *Confronting the Cherry Spirit*,
1834, woodblock print

Caught between two warriors, the Cherry Spirit
leaps through a torchlight held by the one on
the right; all else falls into shadow. The clever
dramatic lighting visually transports the viewer
to the stage to witness the climax of the performance. **XW**

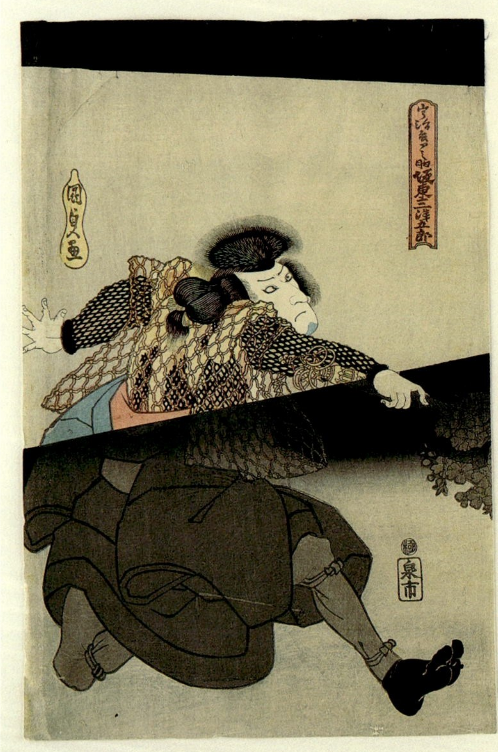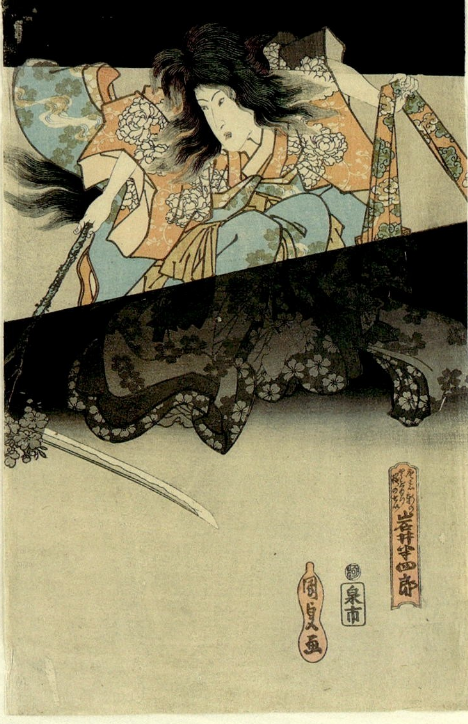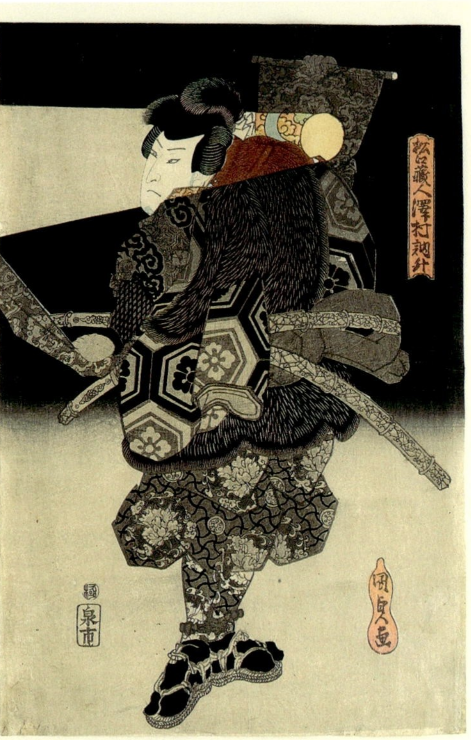

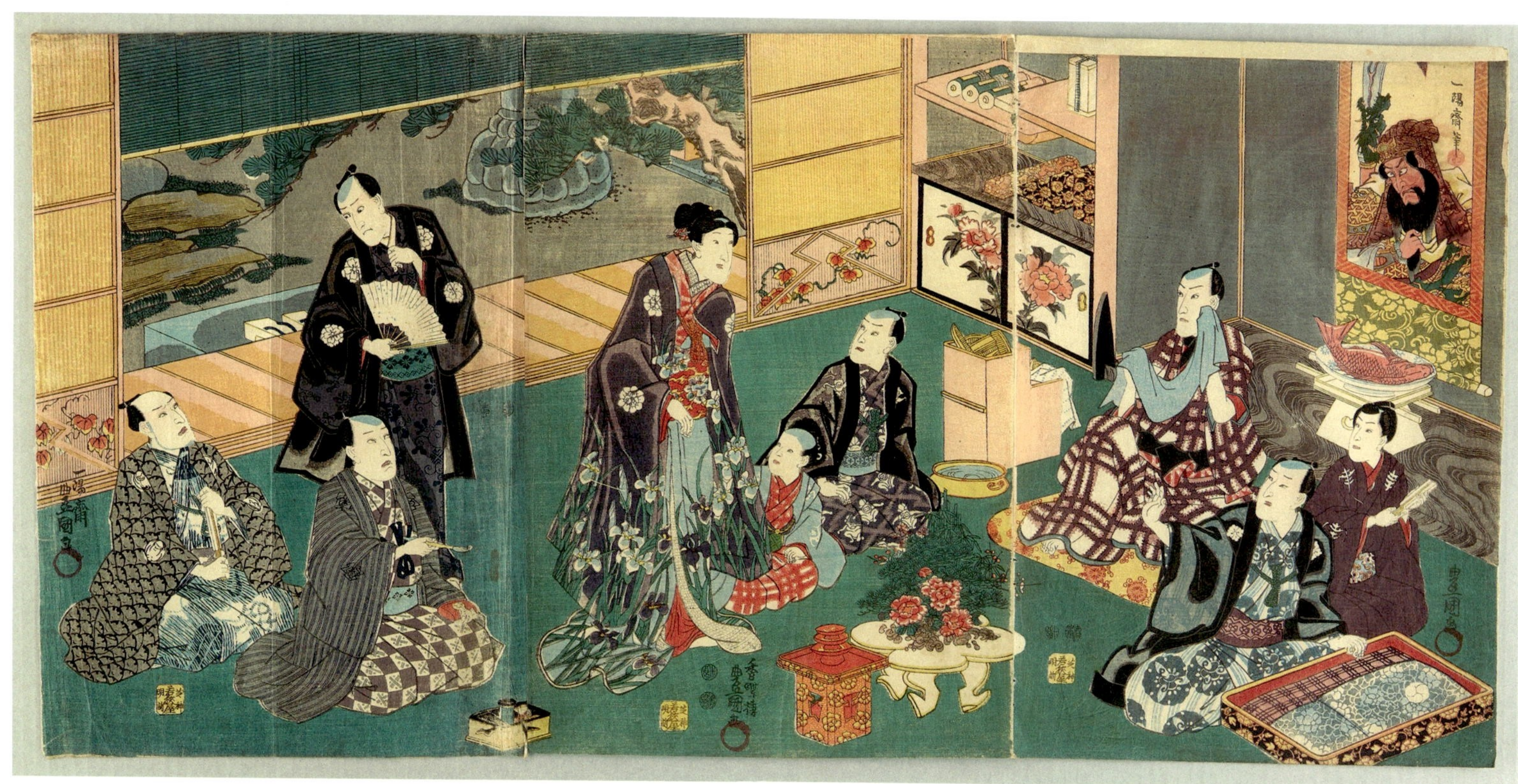

35

PLATE 9
Suzuki Harunobu, *A Dancer Performing Heron Maiden*, ca. 1766–68, woodblock print

The story of Heron Maiden was adapted to the Kabuki stage and first performed in Edo in 1762. Here, a dancer dressed as a white heron performs the heron dance as the other three young women play the shamisen (a three-stringed instrument) for a samurai guest. Suzuki Harunobu, whose signature appears on the folding screen behind the shamisen players, is known for his portrayal of youthful beauty. **XW**

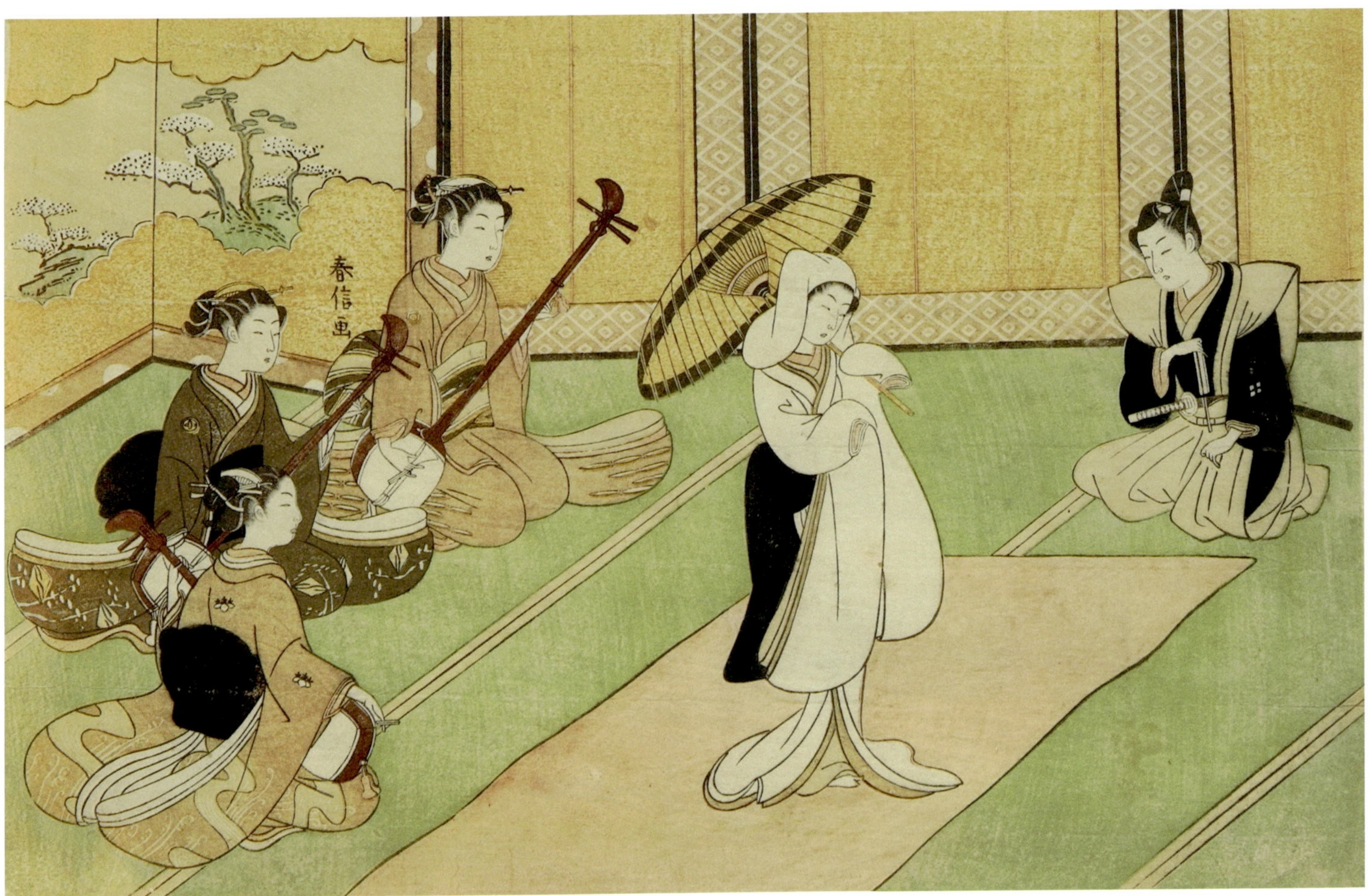

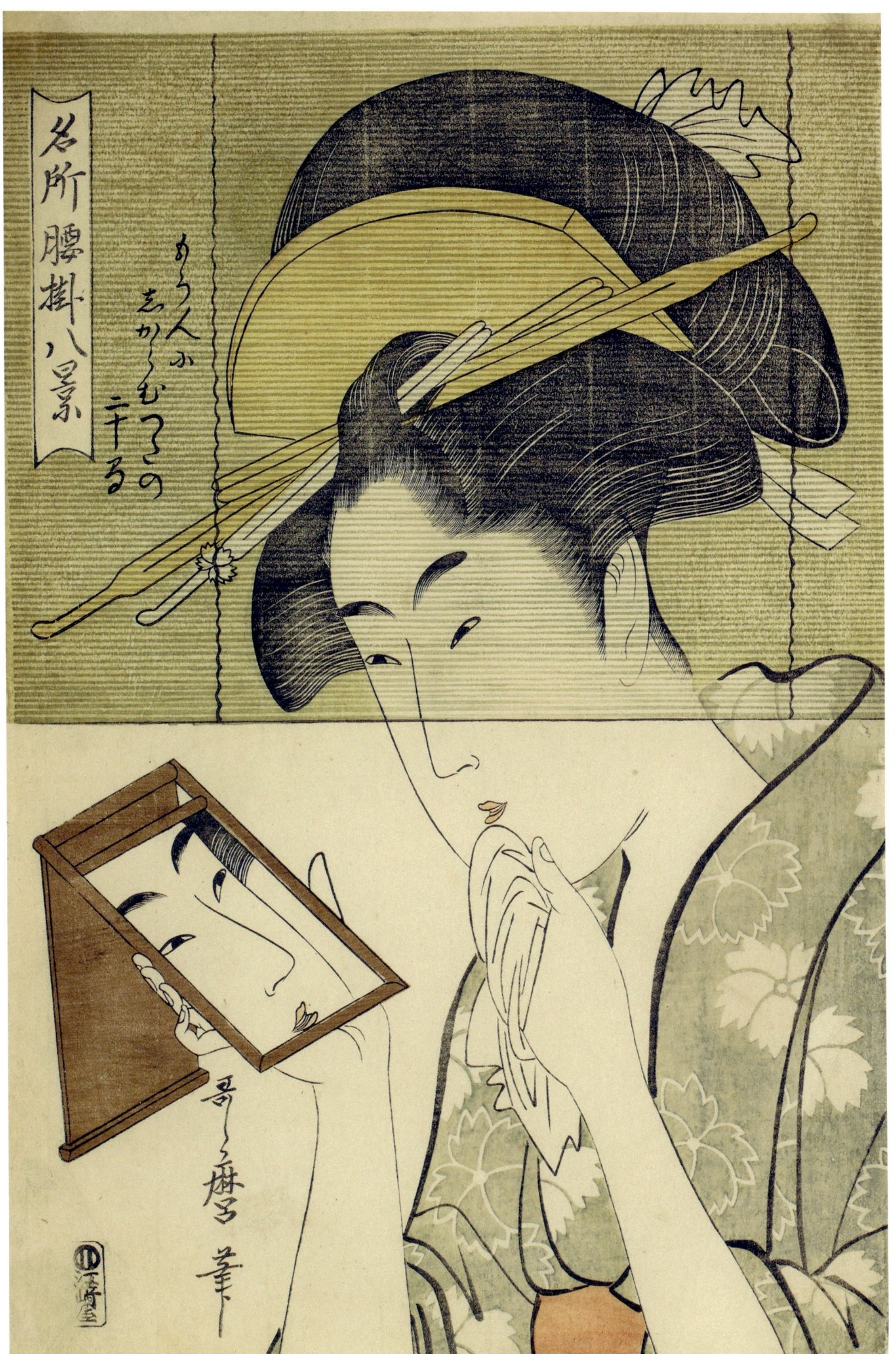

PLATE 10
Kitagawa Utamaro, *Teahouse Waitress behind a Bamboo Blind*, from the series *Eight Views of Tea Stalls in Celebrated Places*, ca. 1795–96, woodblock print

In this print from the series *Eight Views of Tea Stalls in Celebrated Places*, a waitress looks at a mirror—a device Kitagawa Utamaro often used to capture the state of mind of the sitter. The upper half of the print is seen through a bamboo blind, adding an intriguing veil to the face. **XW**

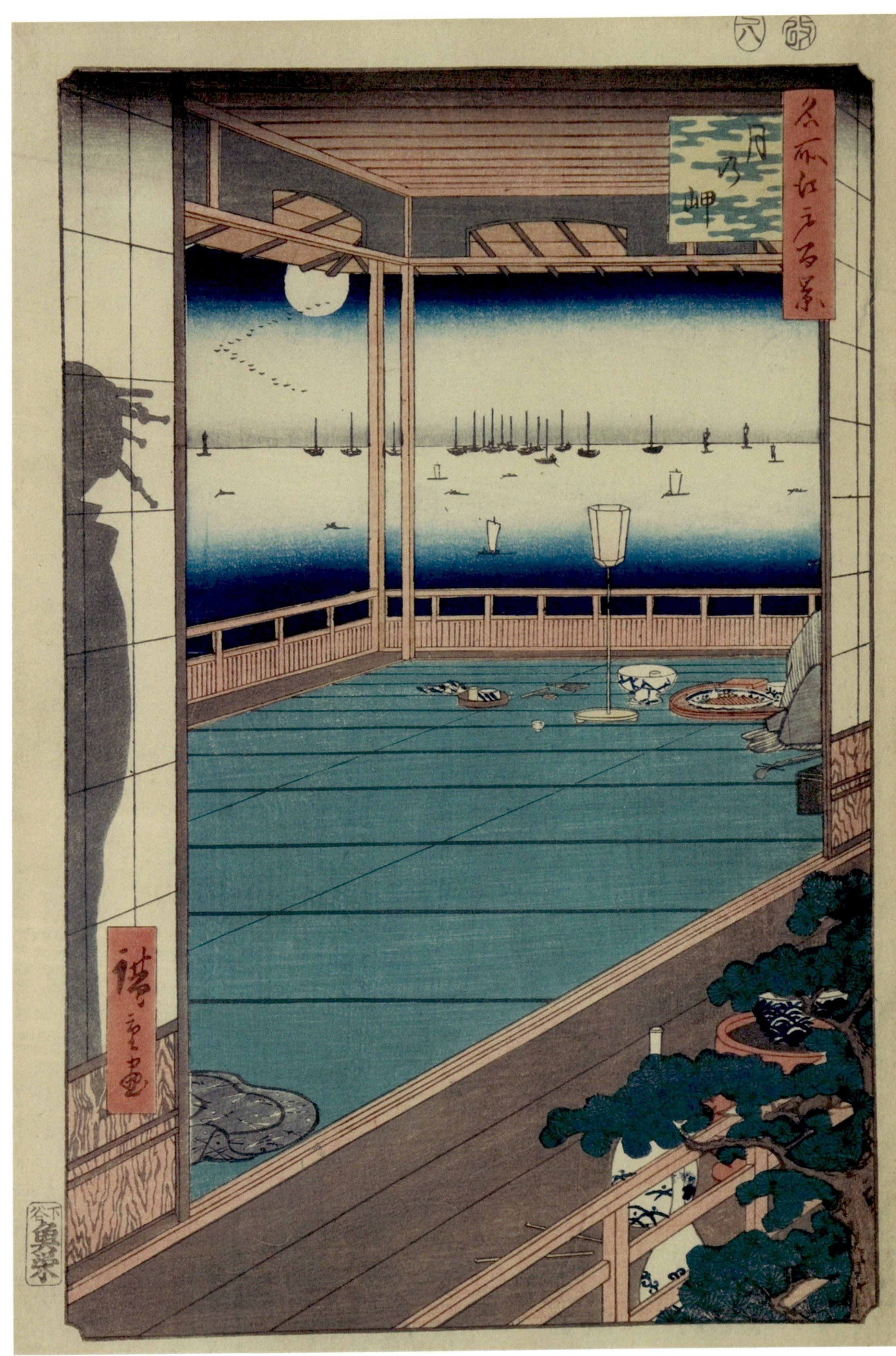

名所江戸百景
月乃岬
廣重画

Utagawa Hiroshige, *Moon Cape*, from the series
One Hundred Views of Famous Places in Edo, 1857,
woodblock print

From Utagawa Hiroshige's celebrated series *One
Hundred Views of Famous Places in Edo*, this print
presents a silhouette of a female figure at the
edge of the picture, provoking the viewer to imag-
ine what might be happening in the room. In the
background is a moonlit view of Edo Bay. **XW**

Utagawa Yoshitora, *Fashionable Spring Moon*,
ca. 1847–52, woodblock print

Silhouettes of a dancer and three musicians can
be seen through the sliding doors, as the three
waitresses in the hallway are busy running errands.
The use of shadow is a compositional element also
found in Henri de Toulouse-Lautrec's work. **XW**

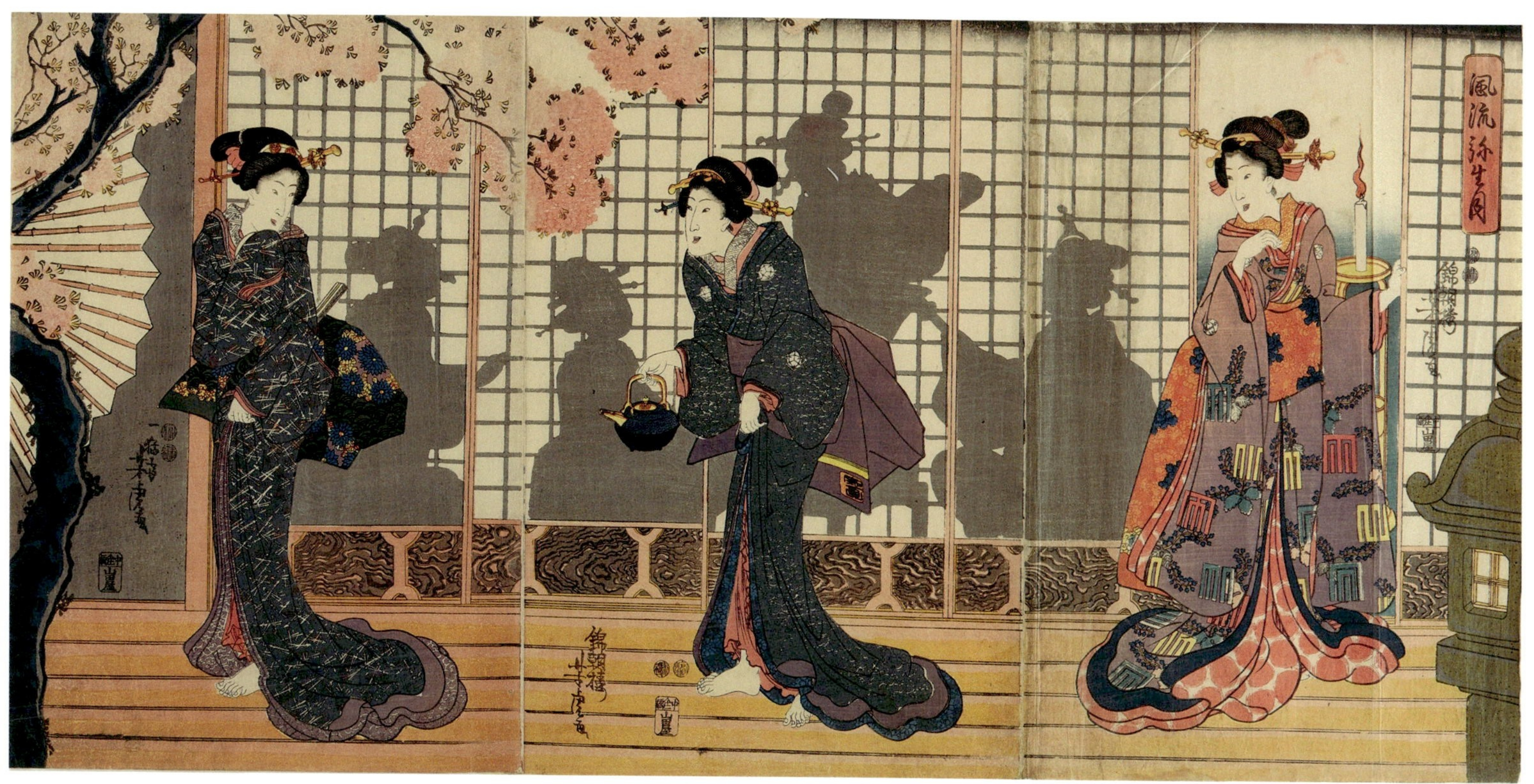

PLATE 13
Henri de Toulouse-Lautrec, *Moulin Rouge: La Goulue*, 1891, color lithograph

Henri de Toulouse-Lautrec made his name overnight with this monumental and highly original poster. The dramatic perspective, bold use of flattened planes of color, and silhouetted spectators (reminiscent of the popular shadow theater) all nod to the influence of ukiyo-e woodcuts on the young French artist. **MWC**

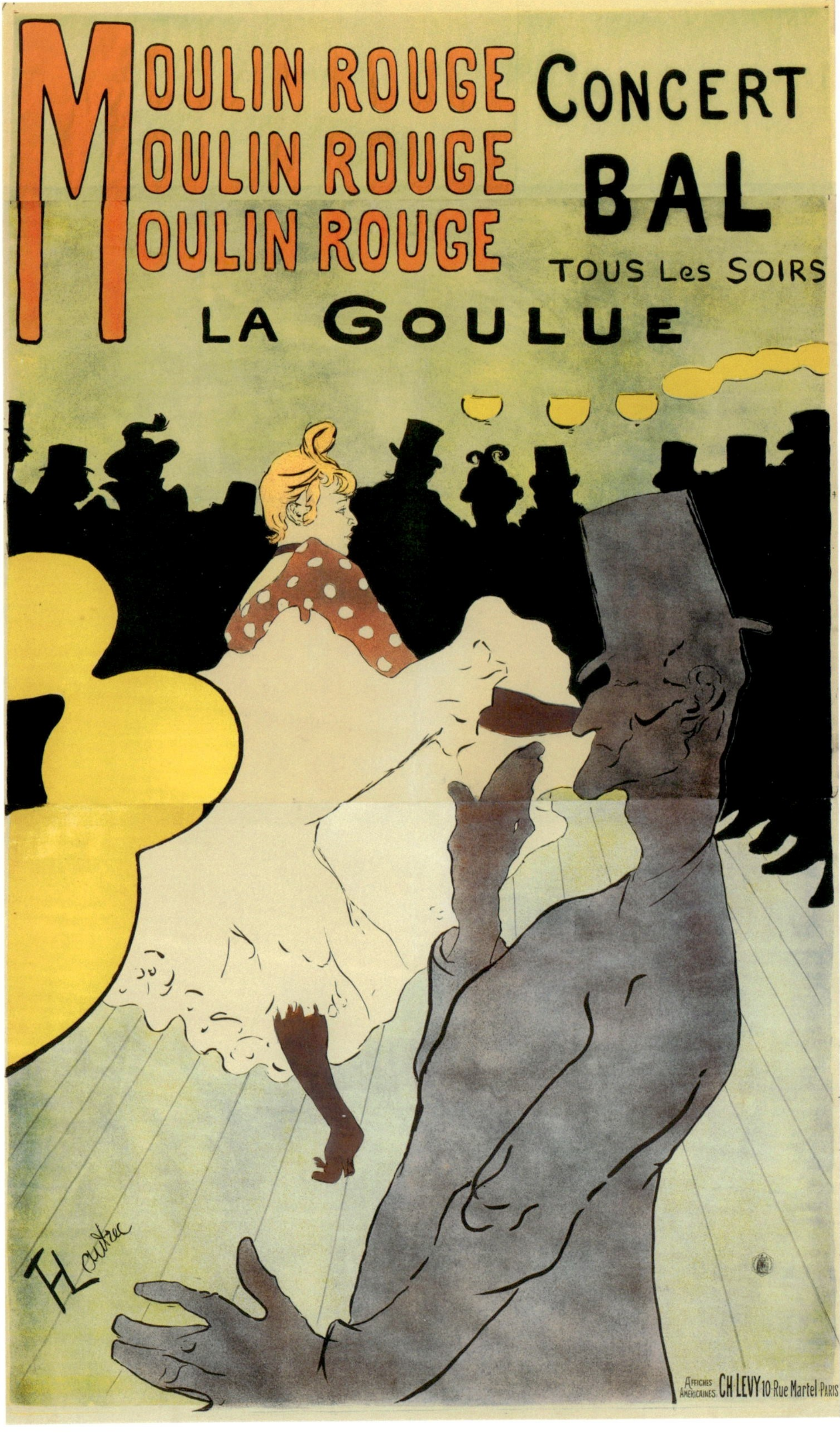

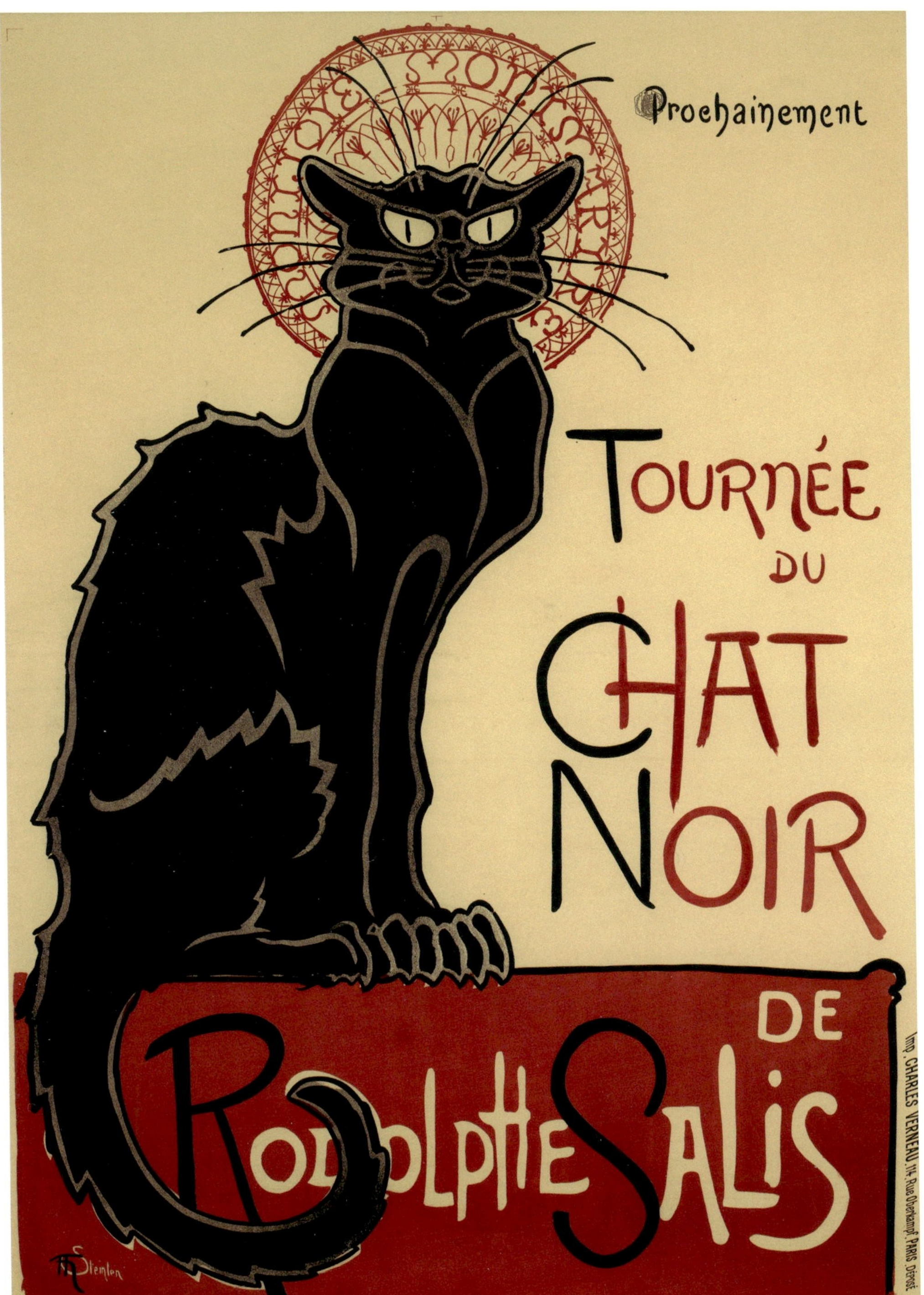

PLATE 14
Théophile Alexandre Steinlen, *Tour of the Chat Noir*, 1896, color lithograph

The Chat Noir cabaret was at the heart of bohemian Montmartre. Founded in 1881, it attracted artists, poets, and playwrights as well as the upper classes of Parisian society, who flocked to hear the latest chansonniers and view productions of the shadow theater. **MWC**

PLATE 15
Henri de Toulouse-Lautrec, *The Englishman at the Moulin Rouge*, 1892, color lithograph

The Moulin Rouge was equally famous as a dance hall and a cruising ground for prostitutes and their eager clients. In this dazzling lithograph—among the first of Henri de Toulouse-Lautrec's career—an Englishman leans forward to proposition two French beauties. **MWC**

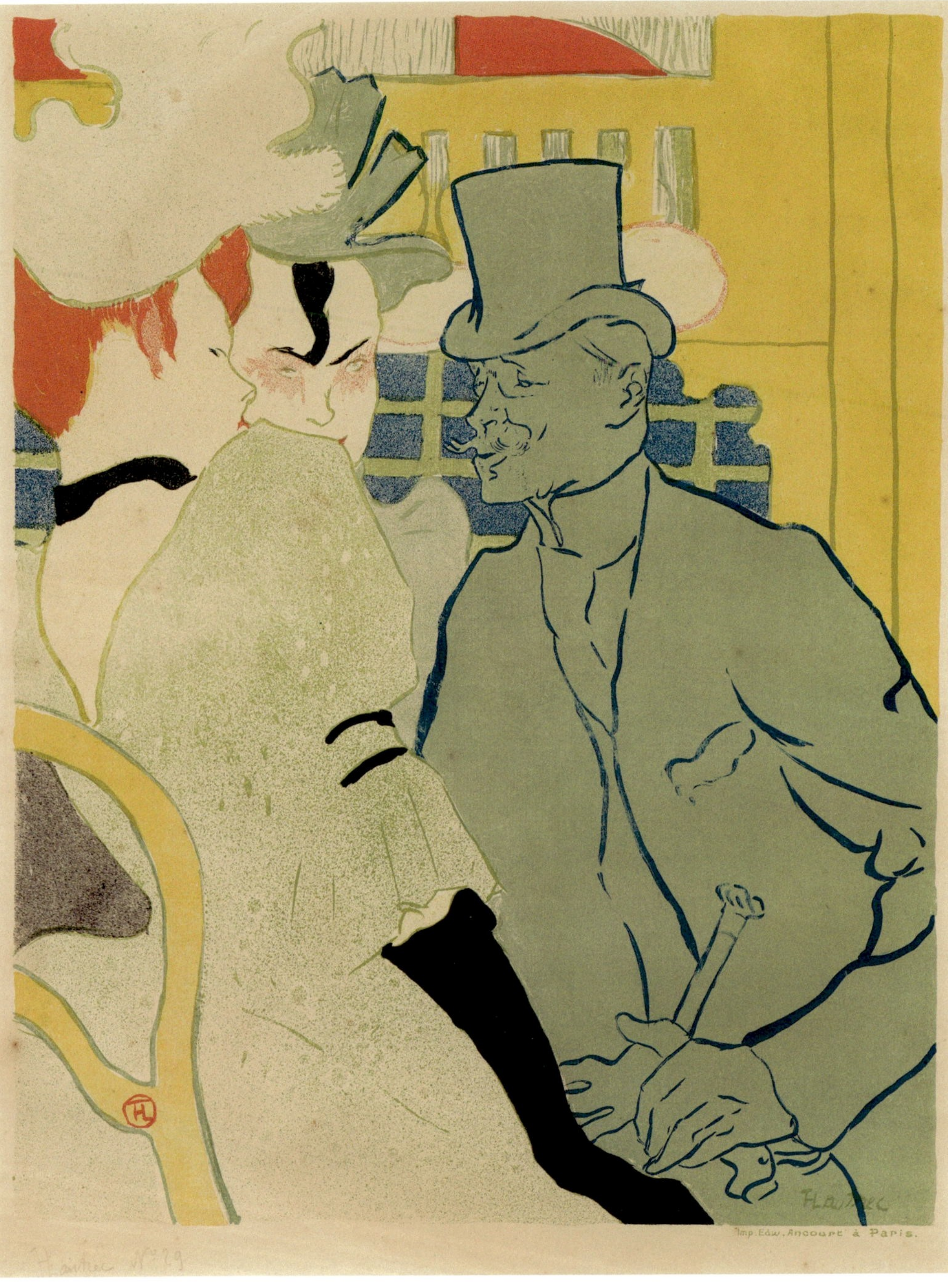

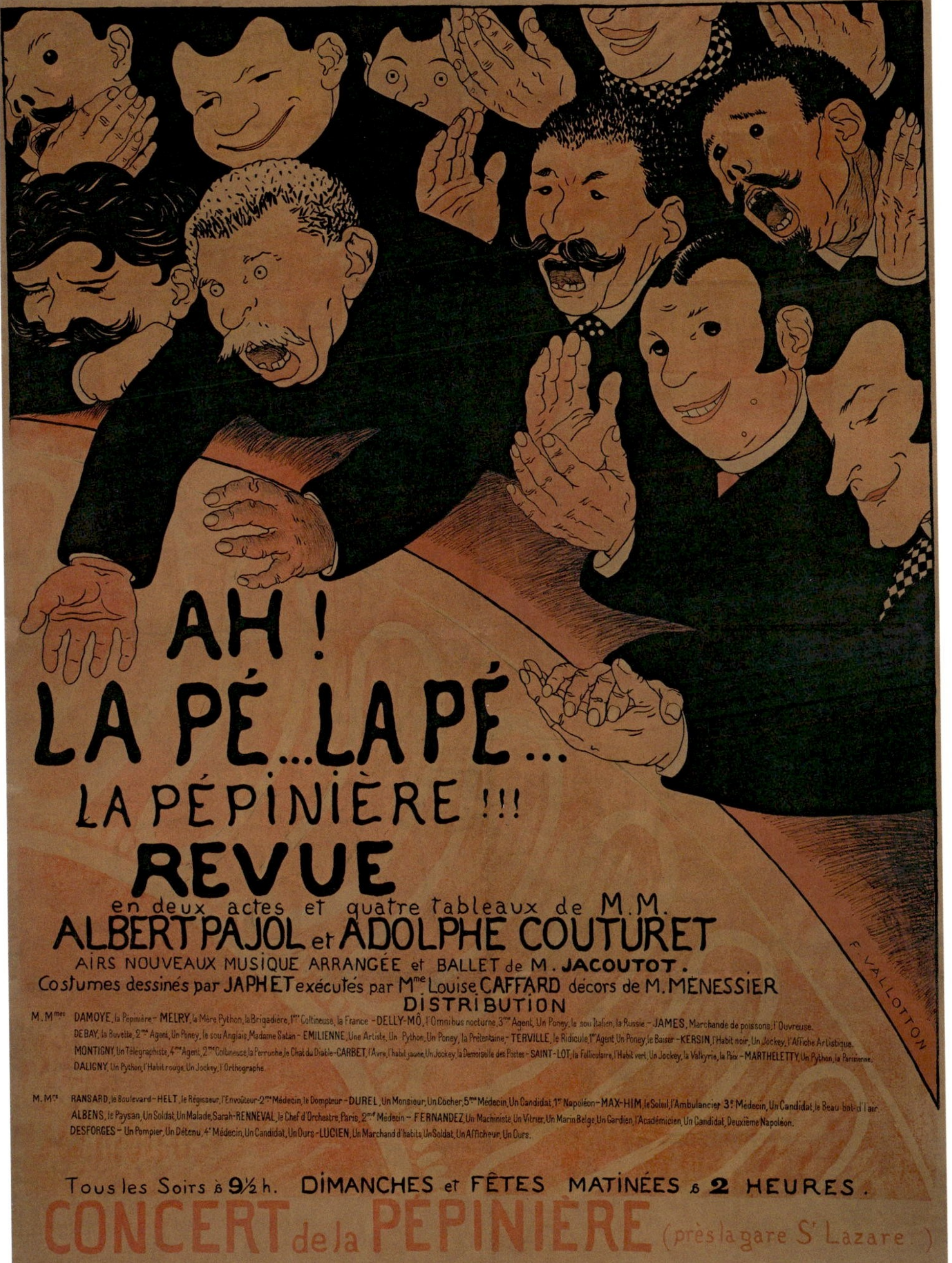

AH !
LA PÉ...LA PÉ...
LA PÉPINIÈRE !!!
REVUE
en deux actes et quatre tableaux de M.M.
ALBERT PAJOL et ADOLPHE COUTURET
AIRS NOUVEAUX MUSIQUE ARRANGÉE et BALLET de M. JACOUTOT.
Costumes dessinés par JAPHET exécutés par Mme Louise CAFFARD décors de M. MÉNESSIER
DISTRIBUTION
M. Mmes DAMOYE, la Pépinière – MELRY, la Mère Python, la Brigadière, 1ère Coltineuse, la France – DELLY-MÔ, l'Omnibus nocturne, 3me Agent, Un Poney, le sou Italien, la Russie – JAMES, Marchande de poissons, l'Ouvreuse.
DEBAY, la Buvette, 2me Agent, Un Poney, le sou Anglais, Madame Satan – EMILIENNE, Une Artiste, Un Python, Un Poney, la Prétentaine – TERVILLE, le Ridicule, 1er Agent, Un Poney, le Baiser – KERSIN, l'Habit noir, Un Jockey, l'Affiche Artistique.
MONTIGNY, Un Télégraphiste, 4me Agent, 2me Coltineuse, la Perruche, le Chat du Diable – CARBET, l'Avre, l'habit jaune, Un Jockey, la Demoiselle des Postes – SAINT-LOT, la Folliculaire, l'Habit vert, Un Jockey, la Valkyrie, la Paix – MARTHELETTY, Un Python, la Parisienne.
DALIGNY, Un Python, l'Habit rouge, Un Jockey, l'Orthographe.

M. Mrs RANSARD, le Boulevard – HELT, le Régisseur, l'Envoûteur-2me Médecin, le Dompteur – DUREL, Un Monsieur, Un Cocher, 5me Médecin, Un Candidat, 1er Napoléon – MAX-HIM, le Soleil, l'Ambulancier, 3e Médecin, Un Candidat, le Beau bat-d'l air.
ALBENS, le Paysan, Un Soldat, Un Malade, Sarah-RENNEVAL, le Chef d'Orchestre, Paris, 2me Médecin – FERNANDEZ, Un Machiniste, Un Vitrier, Un Marin Belge, Un Gardien, l'Académicien, Un Candidat, Deuxième Napoléon.
DESFORGES – Un Pompier, Un Détenu, 4e Médecin, Un Candidat, Un Ours – LUCIEN, Un Marchand d'habits, Un Soldat, Un Afficheur, Un Ours.

Tous les Soirs à 9½ h. DIMANCHES et FÊTES MATINÉES à 2 HEURES.
CONCERT de la PÉPINIÈRE (près la gare St Lazare)
PAJOL & Cie ÉDITEURS, 27, Rue Bergère.
F. VALLOTTON

PLATE 17
Henri de Toulouse-Lautrec, Program cover for the
play *L'Argent* (Money), 1895, color lithograph

In addition to being a dedicated audience member, Henri de Toulouse-Lautrec created several
designs for programs of the avant-garde theaters
he frequented. This image was for the play *L'Argent*
(Money). Although the production was billed as a
comedy in four acts, he suggests a tense moment
between a glowering woman and a hastily retreat-
ing gentleman. **MWC**

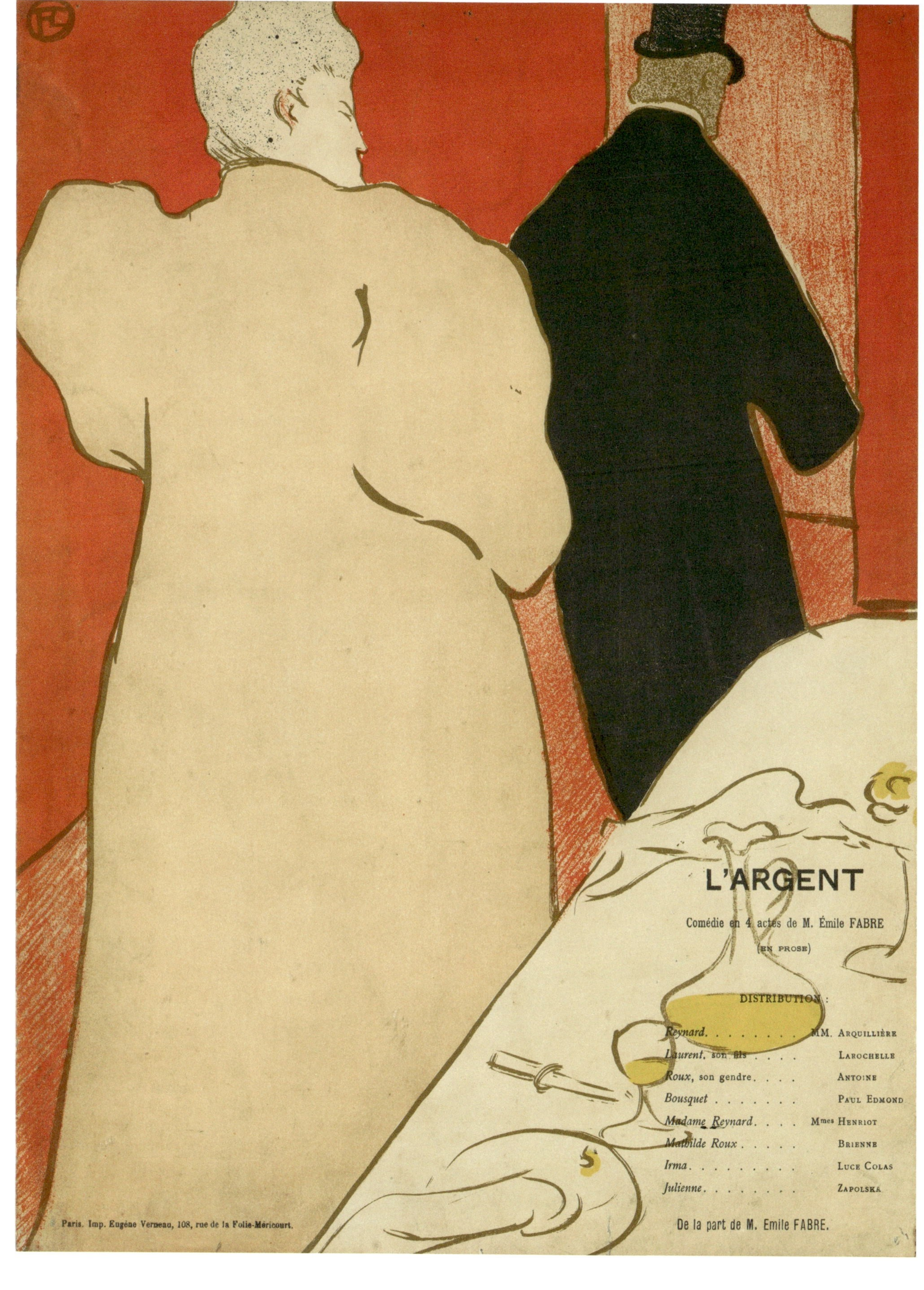

L'ARGENT
Comédie en 4 actes de M. Émile FABRE
(EN PROSE)
DISTRIBUTION :
Reynard. . . . . MM. ARQUILLIÈRE
Laurent, son fils . . . . LAROCHELLE
Roux, son gendre . . . . ANTOINE
Bousquet . . . . PAUL EDMOND
Madame Reynard. . . . Mmes HENRIOT
Mathilde Roux . . . . . BRIENNE
Irma . . . . LUCE COLAS
Julienne . . . . ZAPOLSKA
De la part de M. Emile FABRE.
Paris. Imp. Eugène Verneau, 108, rue de la Folie-Méricourt.

Celebrity Culture

With the rise in popularity of Kabuki theater in Edo, its actors also rose to stardom. Kabuki fans included both men and women; in fact, the latter made up the majority of the audience by the eighteenth century. Aficionados could identify the actors in prints by their family crest or characteristic expressions. For example, generations of actors from the Ichikawa family were often identifiable by their crest composed of three nested squares [23]. Katsukawa Shunshō (1726–1792), an artist best known for his prints of actors, was able to draw out their idiosyncrasies, enabling the viewer to identify the subject [20].[1] Famed actor Ichikawa Danjūrō V had small eyes, closely set beside a large nose. In the print of Danjūrō V in the role of the samurai Arakawa Tarō, Shunshō portrayed him in profile with crossed eyes—a signature expression of Danjūrō in "rough stuff" (*aragoto*) roles—and dressed in a crimson-colored robe featuring his eye-catching crest [23]. Shunshō and other artists also successfully captured the Kabuki's distinctive *onnagata* role, in which a specialist male actor plays female characters [19, 20]. Only male actors were permitted in Kabuki theater from 1629, when the government banned women from performing, out of concern for fans' licentious behavior toward them, giving rise to *onnagata*.

While the biography of Tōshūsai Sharaku (active 1794–95) remains shrouded in mystery, his actor prints have left us with many mesmerizing impressions. He often exaggerated the physical features of stars in his unflattering portrayals [18], just as Henri de Toulouse-Lautrec (1864–1901) did for Yvette Guilbert, who once exclaimed, "For heaven's sake, don't make me so horribly ugly!"[2] Toulouse-Lautrec created numerous works of Guilbert. Among them, two albums of lithographs captured her iconic image with black-gloved arms, a thrust-out chin, and a hooked nose. Toulouse-Lautrec was a master of grasping the characteristics that made a person recognizable: La Goulue's squinty eyes and red topknot, Aristide Bruant's black hat and red scarf, and Jane Avril's bonnet and erratic dance moves.

In Paris, the idea of a celebrity was evolving in the late nineteenth century. For example, the cancan dancer La Goulue [29], among other luminaries of Montmartre, rose to fame not because she was born into a prominent family, but because she was able to attract the limelight. Toulouse-Lautrec came onto the scene at a timely moment, just as celebrity culture was changing. Through his posters, widely distributed throughout the streets of Paris, he promoted entertainers to celebrity status, and along the way became one himself, coming to symbolize Montmartre.[3] Similarly, Japanese print artists such as Kitagawa Utamaro (1753–1806) and Sharaku also became well known through the promotion of publishers. Poetry groups, Kabuki fan clubs, and brothel owners sponsored the production of their prints; the range of work the artists were able to secure, from commercial prints to theater playbills and programs to travel guidebooks, increased their celebrity.[4]

In both Edo and Paris, though at different times, the emergence of celebrity culture accompanied an ascendant bourgeoisie's challenge to the established social order, and the widening circulation and active collecting of printed materials contributed to the construction of celebrity. **XW**

NOTES

1. Timothy Clark, "Katsukawa Shunshō," in Meech, Oliver, and Carpenter, *Designed for Pleasure*, 110–12.

2. Letter from Guilbert to Toulouse-Lautrec, reproduced in Maurice Joyant, *Henri de Toulouse-Lautrec* (Paris: H. Floury, 1926; repr., New York: Arno Press, 1968), 146; citation to the Arno Press edition.

3. For a detailed discussion on this subject, see Chapin, "Toulouse-Lautrec and the Culture of Celebrity," in Thomson, Cate, and Chapin, *Toulouse-Lautrec and Montmartre*, 46–63.

4. Davis, *Picturing the Floating World*, 82.

PLATE 18
Tōshūsai Sharaku, *The Actor Sawamura Sōjūrō III as
Kujaku Saburō*, 1794, woodblock print

In less than a year, Tōshūsai Sharaku produced
some of the most iconic images of Kabuki actors.
This half-length portrait of Sōjūrō is no exception.
The face is full of tension, with the lips reduced to
one line; the right hand rests firmly on the sword
as if he is about to pull it out for a fight. **XW**

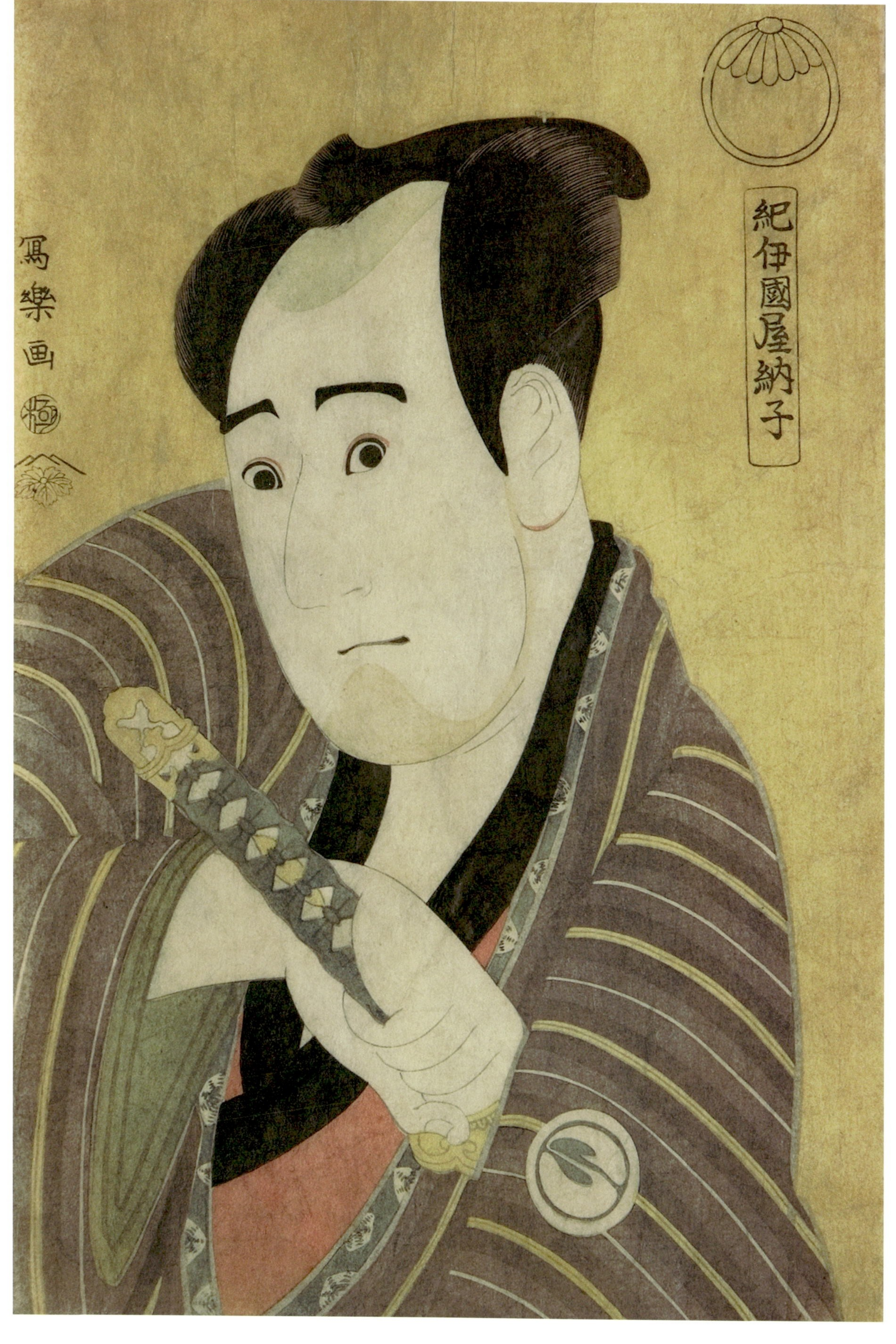
紀伊國屋納子
寫樂画

PLATE 19
Utagawa Kunihisa, *The Actor Segawa Michinosuke in a Female Role*, 1804, woodblock print

In this rare print by Utagawa Kunihisa, the famed *onnagata* (an actor specializing in female roles) Segawa Michinosuke plays the ghost of the *yūjo* Ōshū in a Kabuki play performed at the Ichimura theater in 1804. It was said Ōshū's beauty was so great that it could bring down an empire; the haughty look on the face attests to it. **XW**

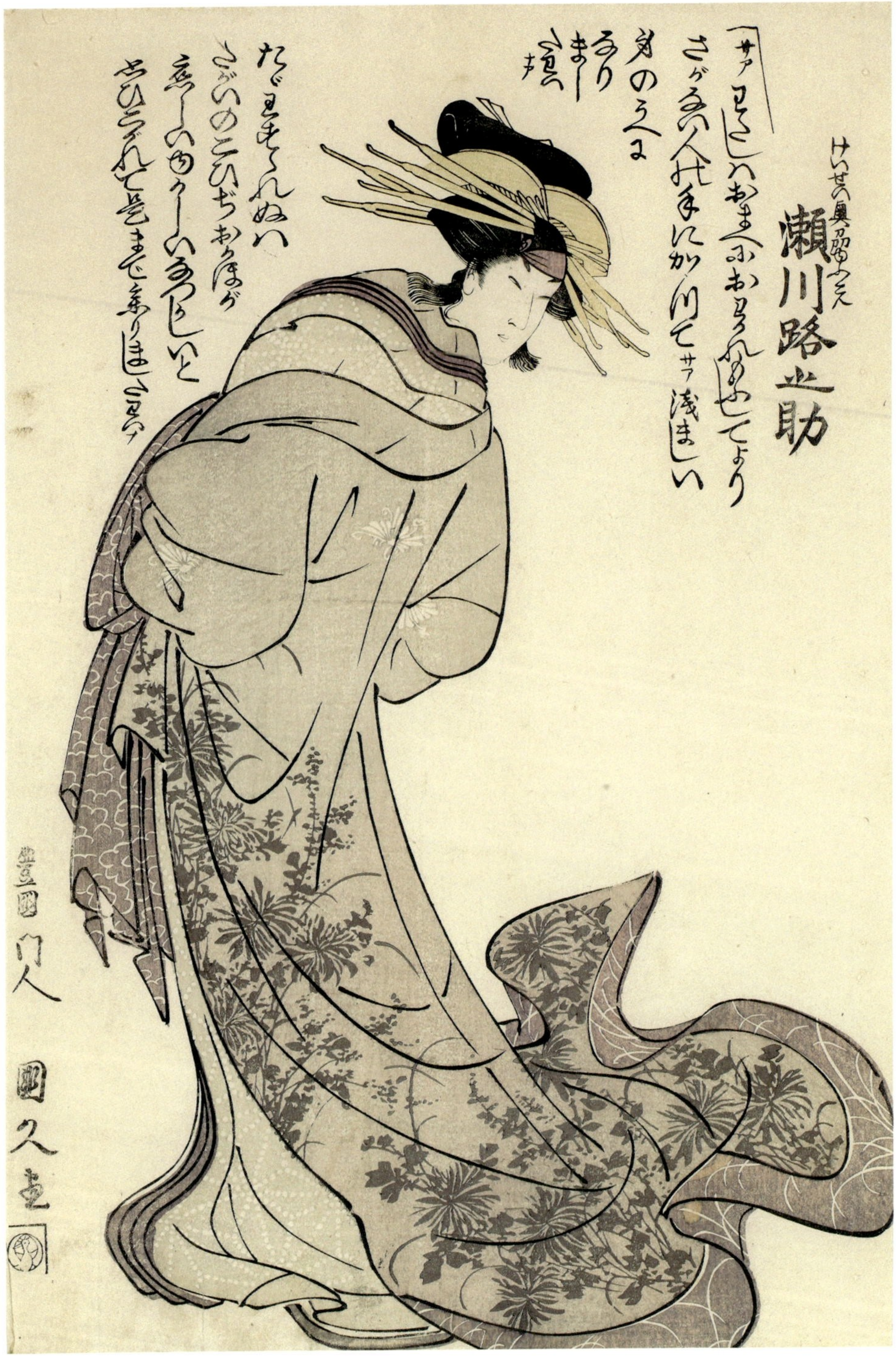

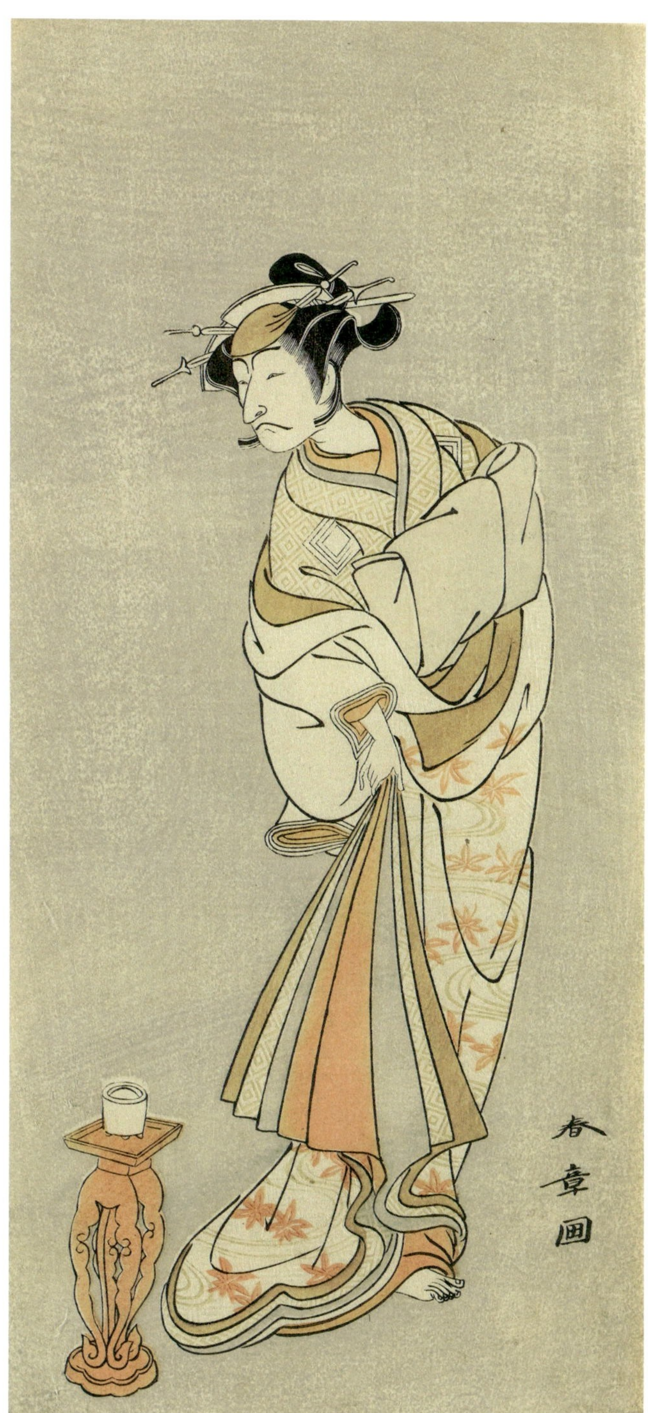

PLATE 20
Katsukawa Shunshō, *The Actor Ichikawa Danjūrō V as the Spirit of Monk Seigen*, 1772, woodblock print

Danjūrō V, who usually played heroic or villainous male characters, is in female guise as the spirit of the monk Seigen in this print. The long, aquiline nose helps the informed viewer identify him. He was performing a dance in the play *Keisei Momiji no Uchikake* (Courtesan in an Over-Kimono of Maple Leaf Pattern), which was onstage at the Morita theater in 1772. The maple leaves on the outer kimono allude to the play. **XW**

PLATE 21
Katsukawa Shunei, *The Actor Ichikawa Danjūrō V*,
1780s, woodblock print

Playing a character with super strength, Danjūrō V,
with his signature persimmon-colored robe tied
around his waist, lifts a large rock above his head.
Like other artists of the Katsukawa school, Shunei
also specialized in actor prints. **XW**

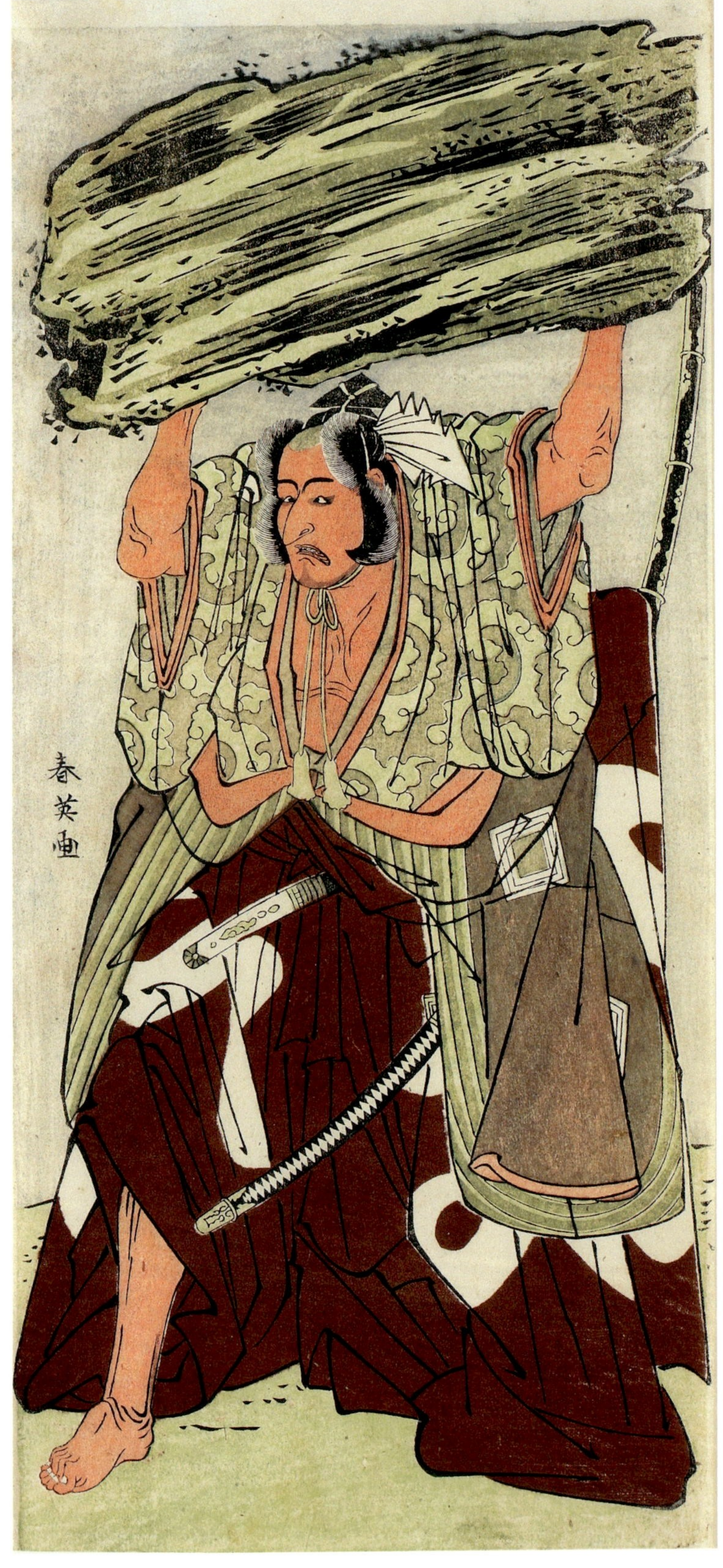

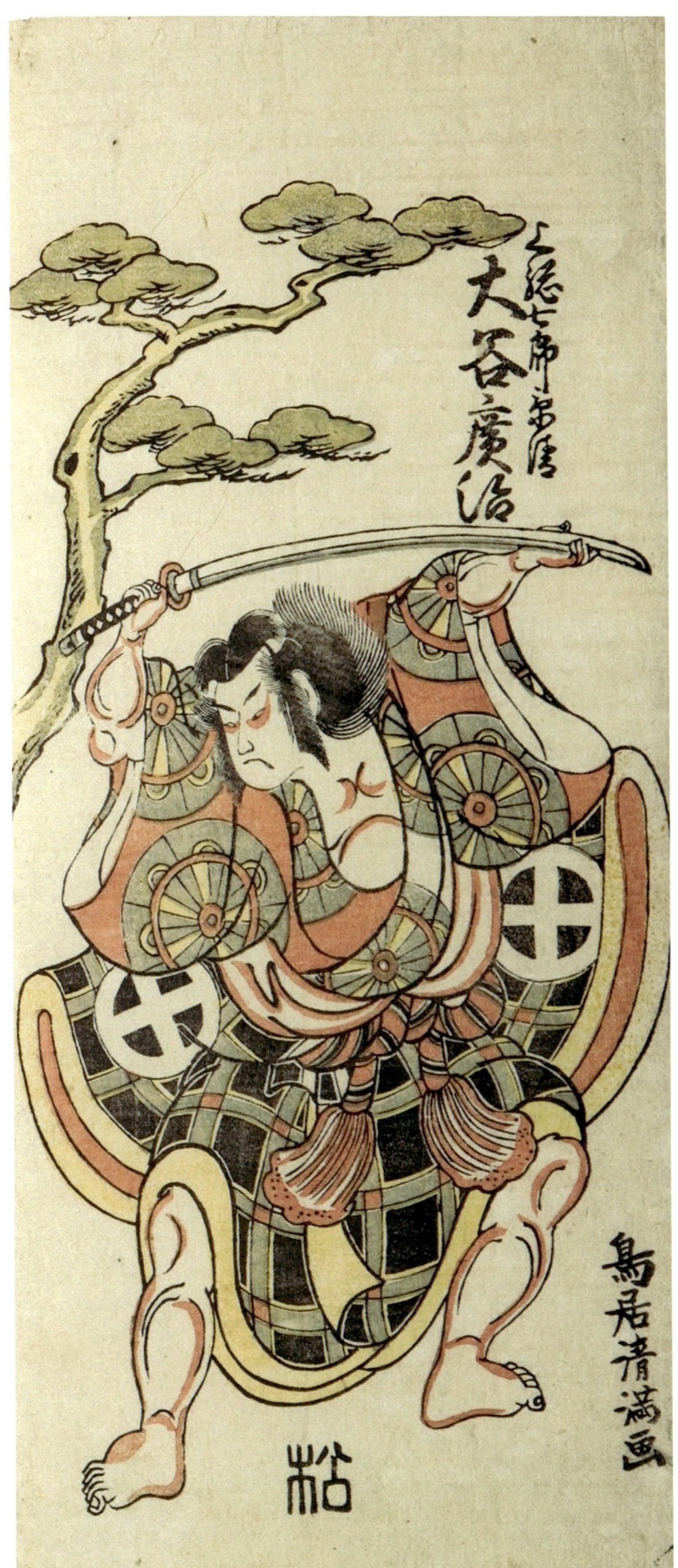

PLATE 22
Torii Kiyomitsu, *The Actor Ōtani Hiroji II as Kazusa no Shichirō Kagekiyo*, ca. 1750, woodblock print

The Torii school was a key contributor to the development of Kabuki actor prints. This example was made with three color blocks—pink, yellow, and green—before full-color printing was invented in 1765. Here, actor Ōtani Hiroji II is imitating the "rough stuff" (*aragoto*) acting style of the famed Danjūrō I. **XW**

PLATE 23
Katsukawa Shunshō, *The Actor Ichikawa Danjūrō V
as Arakawa Tarō*, 1778, woodblock print

In the play *Date Nishiki Tsui no Yumitori* (A Dandy-
ish Brocade: Opposing Warriors) at the Morita
theater in 1778, Danjūrō V played the warrior
Arakawa Tarō. The profile view and the stun-
ning robe in persimmon call to mind Henri de
Toulouse-Lautrec's prints of Aristide Bruant.
The design of three nested squares on Danjūrō's
robe is the Ichikawa family crest. **XW**

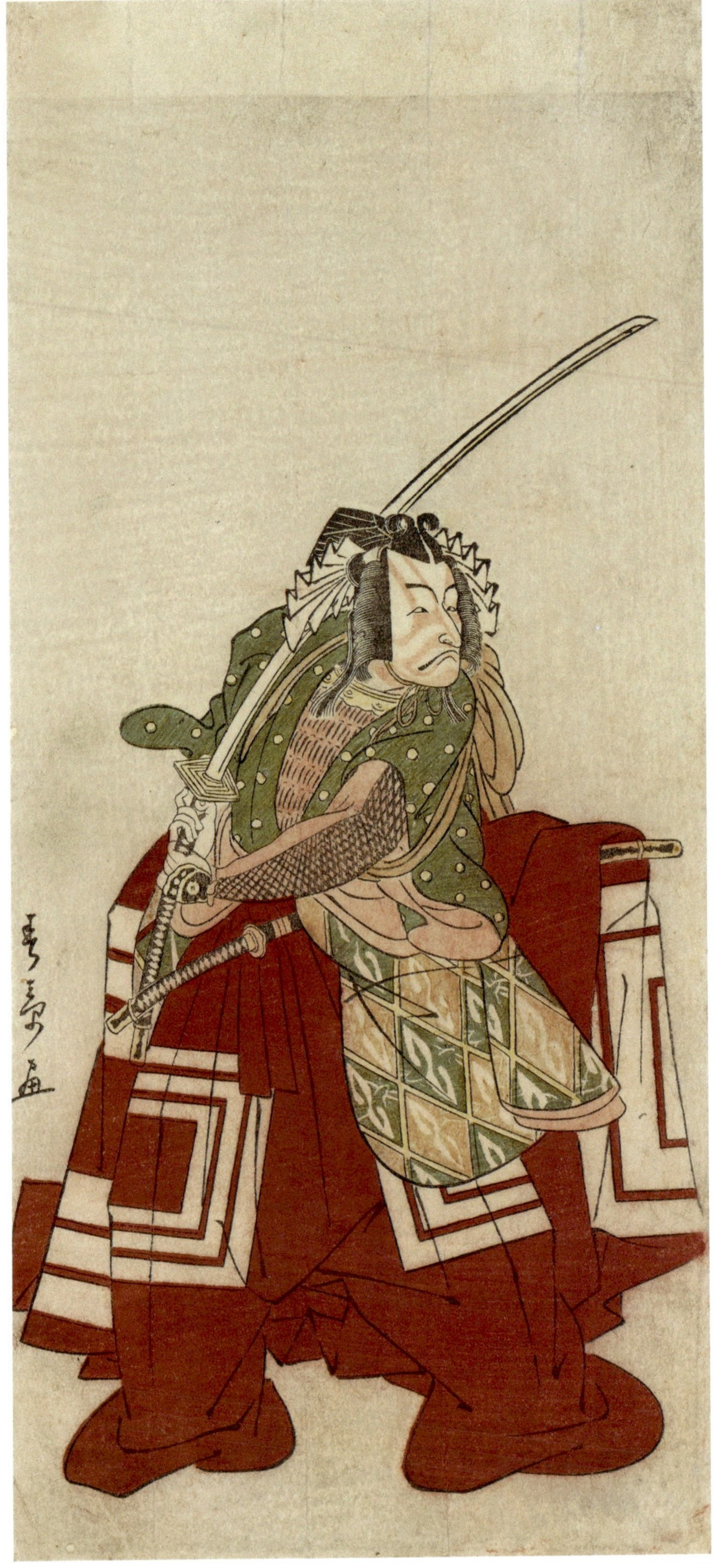

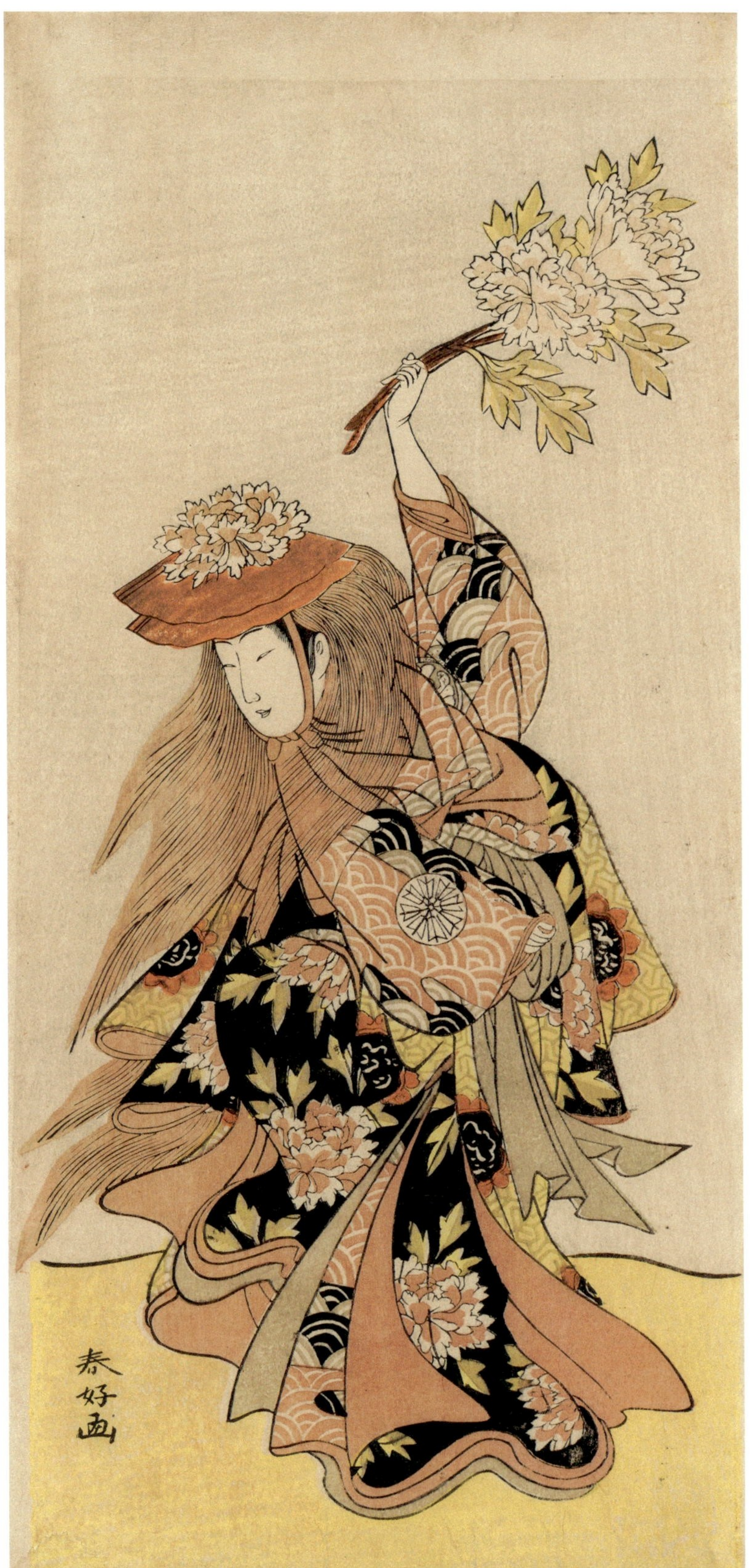

PLATE 24
Katsukawa Shunkō, *The Actor Nakamura Tomijūrō in the Lion Dance*, 1778, woodblock print

In his farewell performance at the Ichimura theater in Edo before his return to western Japan, Nakamura Tomijūrō I (1719–1786) performed a sequence of seven dances, showing off his superb acting skills. Katsukawa Shunkō designed one print for each dance; this one is for the lion dance.
XW

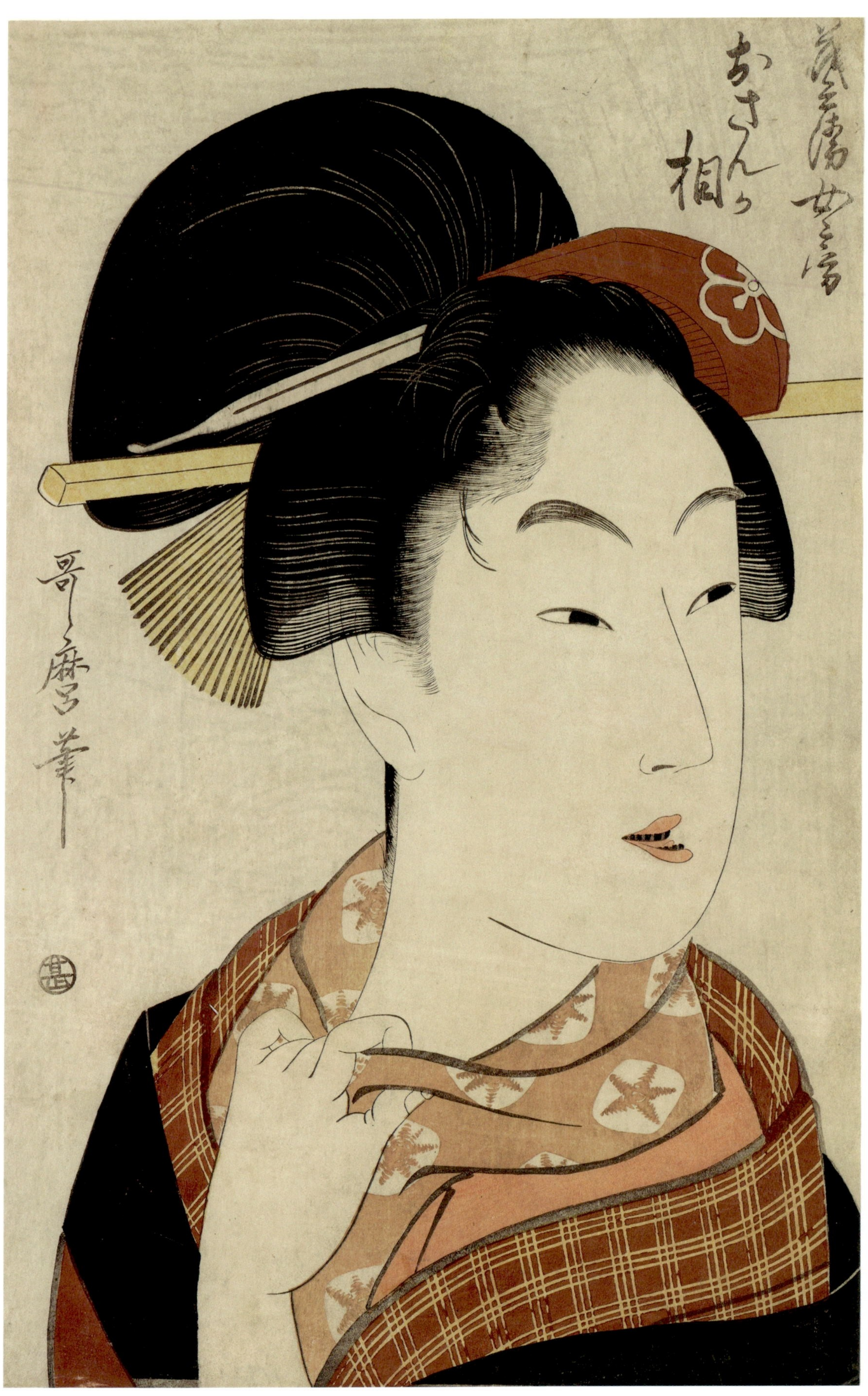

美艶女三笑
おさんの相
哥麿筆

Osan, wife of a head mounter for sutras and paintings at the court in Kyoto, was executed with her lover Mōhei for adultery in 1683. Her widely known story was adapted in the 1686 novel *Five Women Who Loved Love* as well as in a 1715 puppet theater play. Kitagawa Utamaro portrayed Osan as a beauty, as the tale has it; her blackened teeth indicate that she was married. XW

PLATE 26
Kitagawa Utamaro, *Pensive Love*, ca. 1793, woodblock print

A masterwork of Kitagawa Utamaro's, this print
captures the subtle feelings of this woman. She
has shaved her eyebrows, indicating she is married, and looks away as if deep in thought about
an impossible love. The *ookubi* (literally, "big-
head") profile portrait is a signature design of
Utamaro's and a feature that Henri de Toulouse-
Lautrec deftly adapted. **XW**

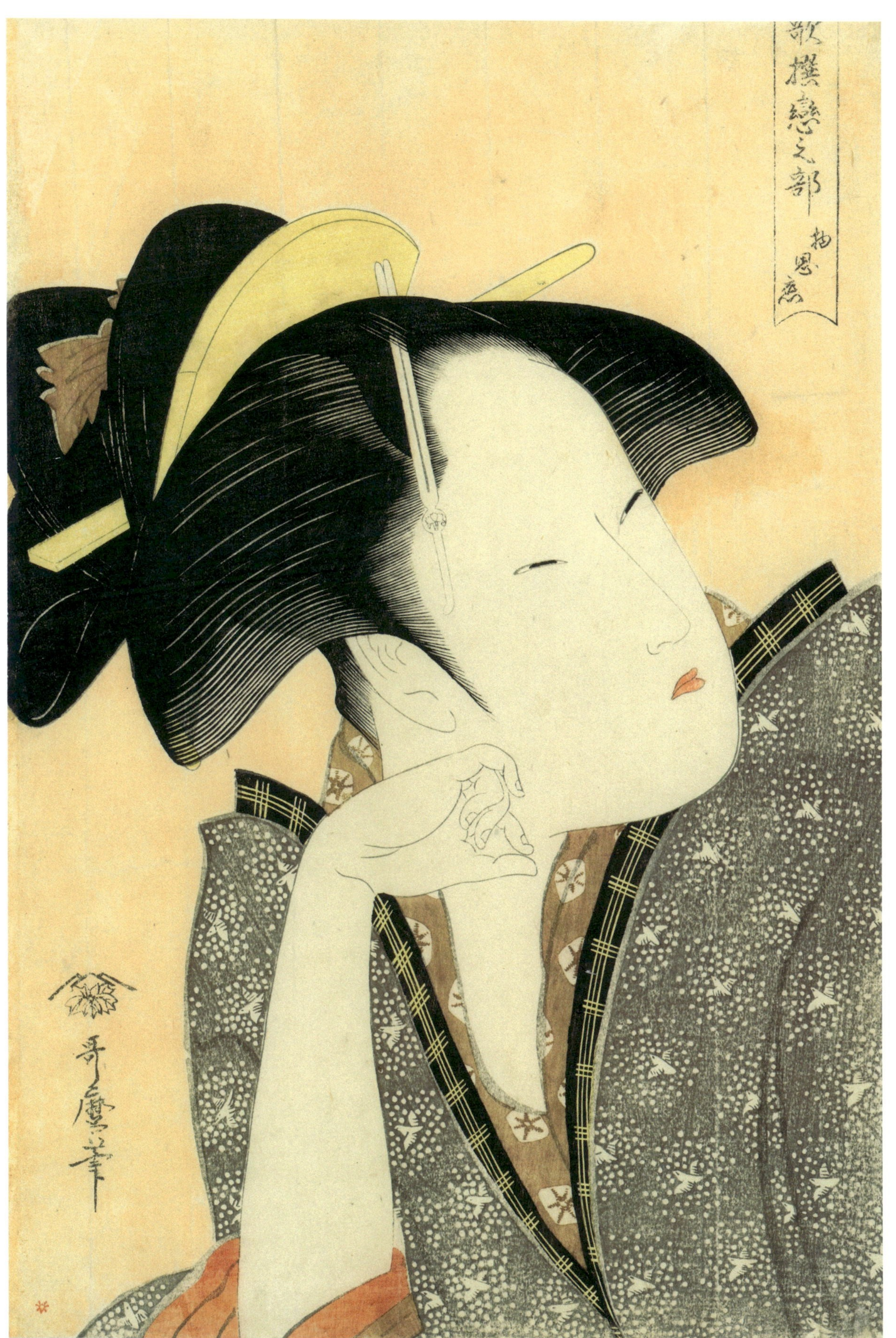

歌撰戀之部
物思戀
歌麿筆

PLATE 27
Henri de Toulouse-Lautrec, *Yvette Guilbert Onstage*, cover for the album *Yvette Guilbert*, 1898, lithograph

Café-concert star Yvette Guilbert was among Henri de Toulouse-Lautrec's favorite models. He delighted in her exaggerated movements, thin proportions, and wry sense of humor. Although she didn't always appreciate his caricatural depictions of her, they shared a mutual respect. This album consists of eight lithographs plus a cover of the *divette* onstage. **MWC**

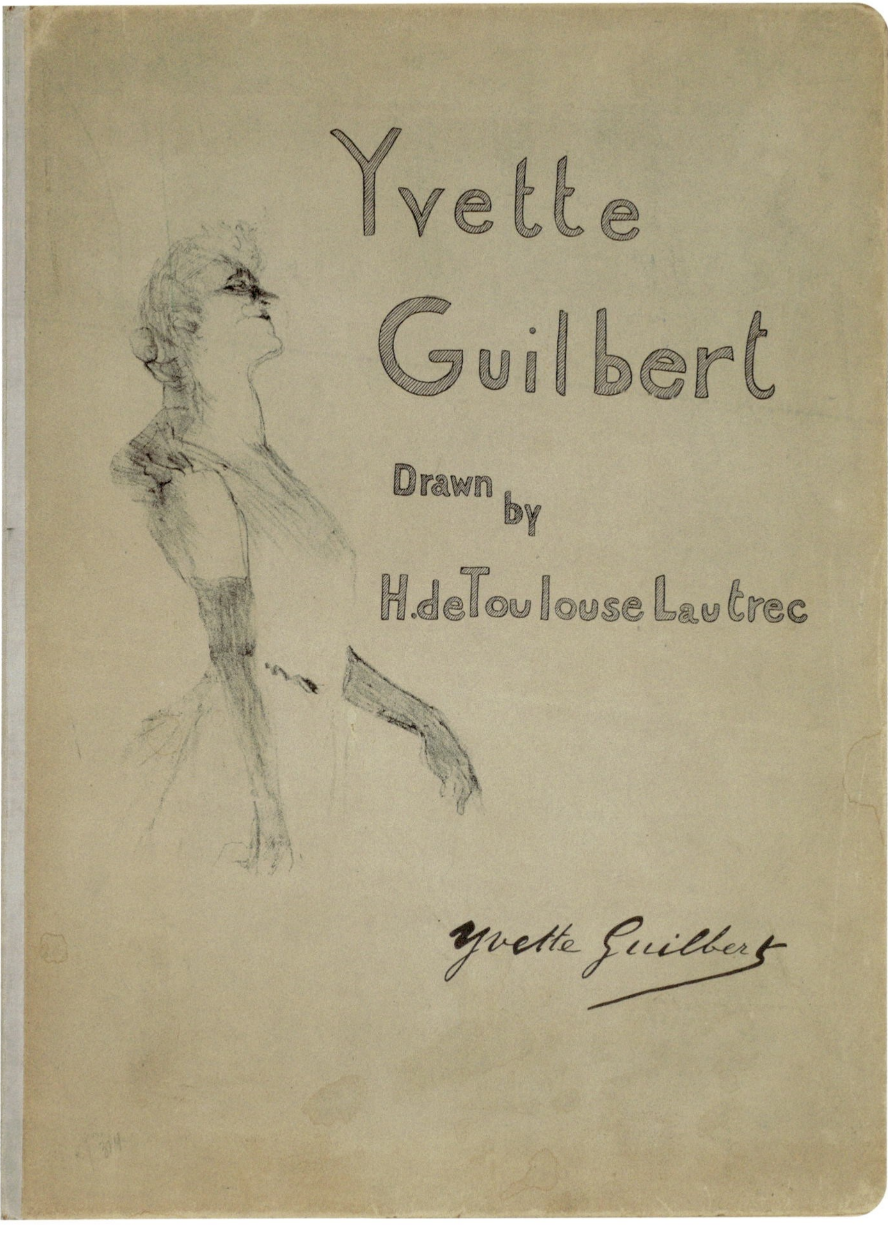

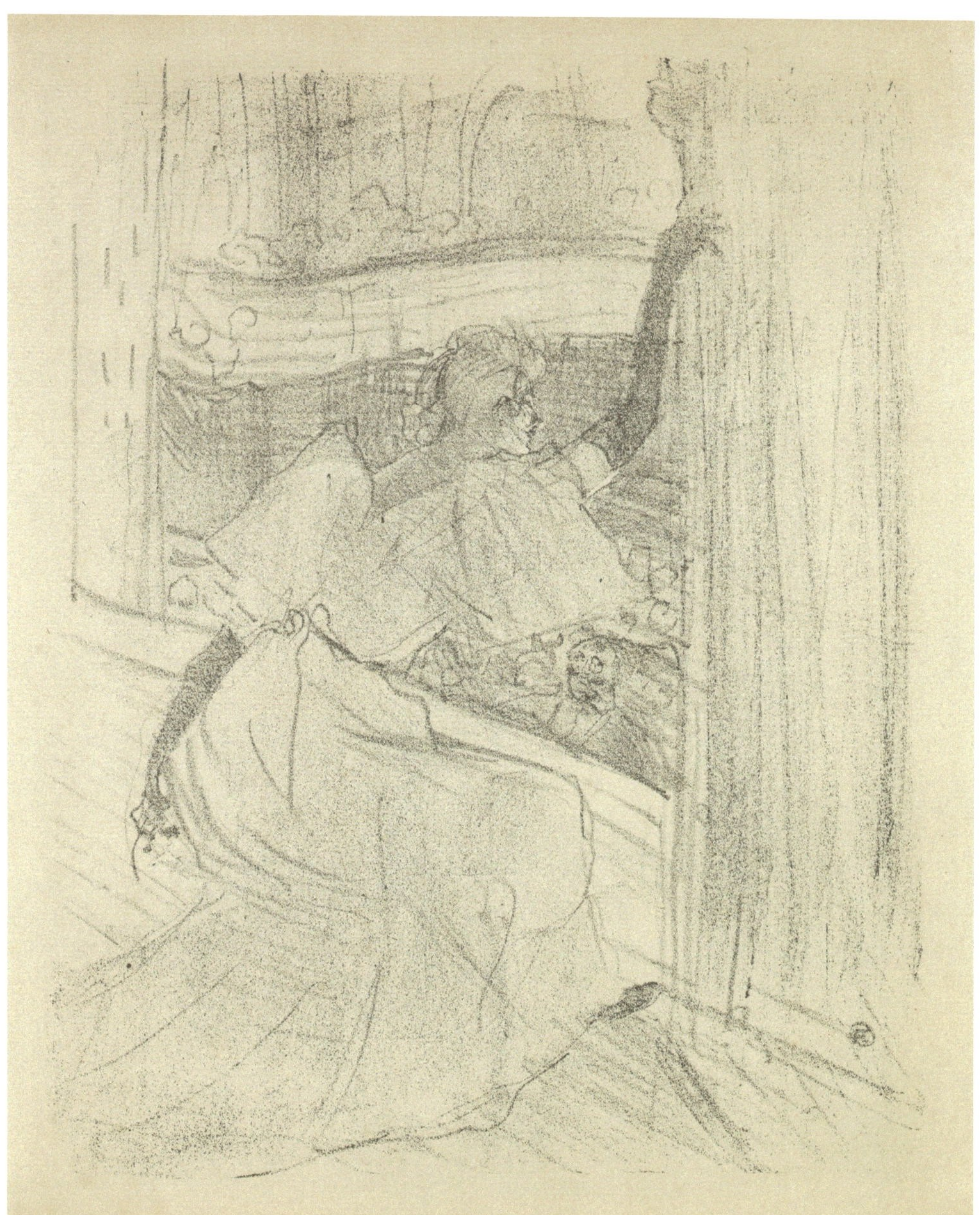

Henri de Toulouse-Lautrec, *Yvette Guilbert Bowing*, from the album *Yvette Guilbert*, 1898, lithograph

Yvette Guilbert was known for her stage costume featuring elbow-length black gloves. Here, Henri de Toulouse-Lautrec attenuated the size and exaggerated the position of her gloved arms to great effect, suggesting the elegance of this lanky performer. **MWC**

PLATE 29
Henri de Toulouse-Lautrec, *At the Moulin Rouge:
La Goulue and Her Sister*, 1892, color lithograph

Born Louise Weber, this famous dancer was
known as La Goulue (the Glutton), a reference
to her voracious appetite for living and her pen-
chant for finishing customers' drinks. The indis-
putable star of the high-kicking cancan, she was
one of Henri de Toulouse-Lautrec's most fre-
quent subjects. Here, she surveys the Moulin
Rouge arm in arm with another woman, sometimes identified as her sister or, alternatively,
her lover. **MWC**

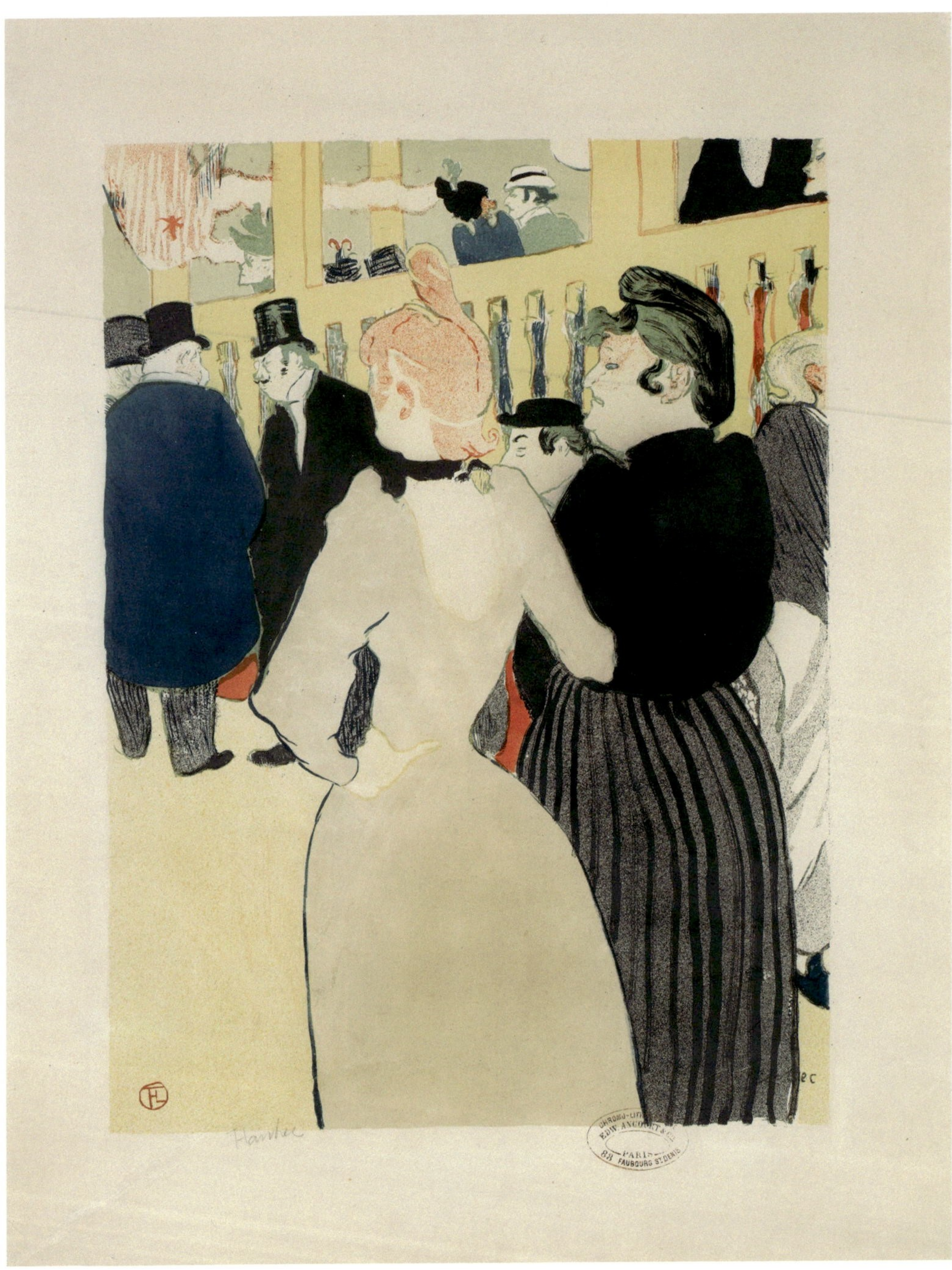

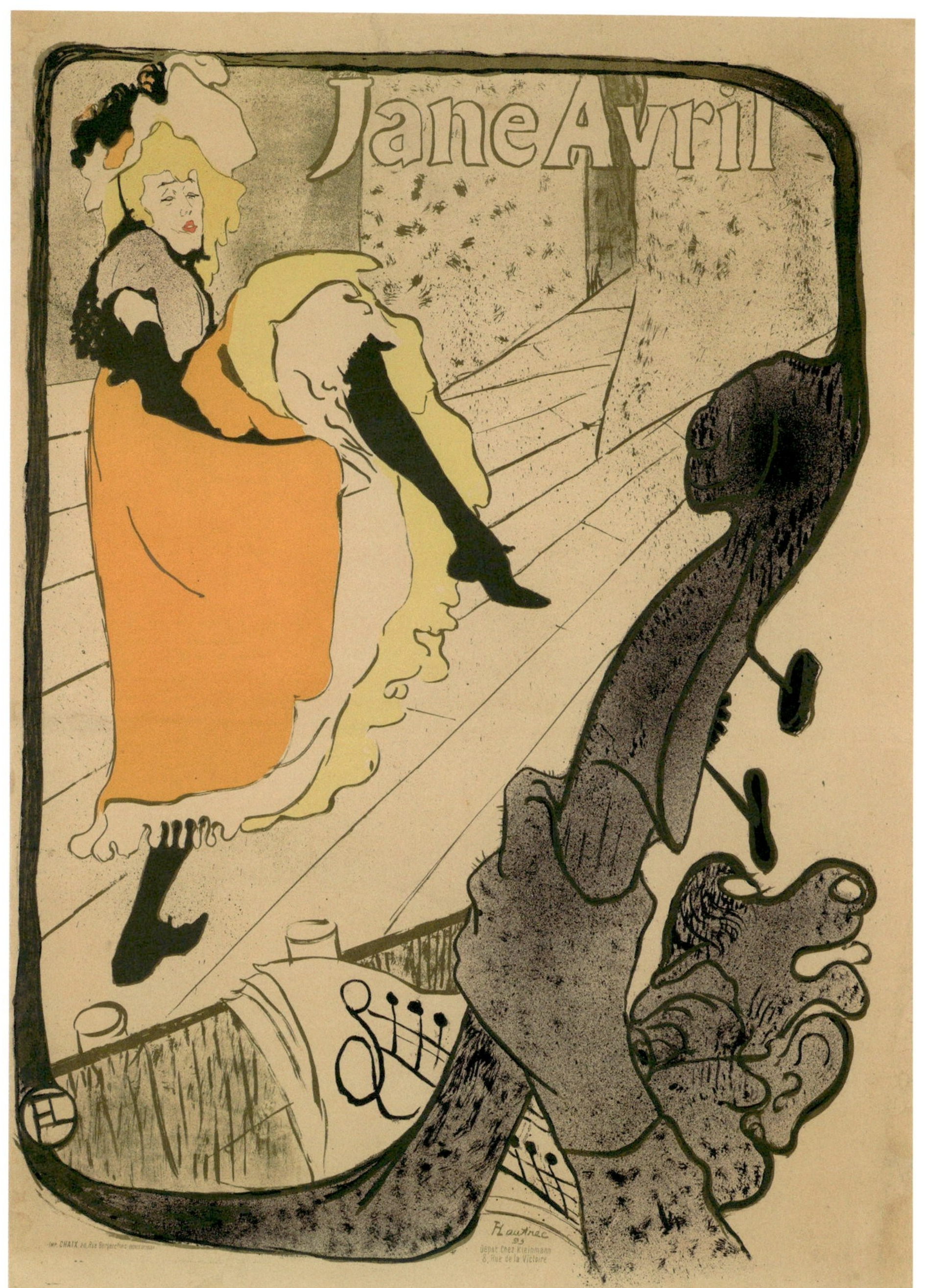

PLATE 30
Henri de Toulouse-Lautrec, *Jane Avril*, 1893, color lithograph

The scroll of the double bass partly frames dancer Jane Avril in this poster for her appearance at the Jardin de Paris, a café-concert on the illustrious Champs-Élysées. Dancers like Avril often performed both in Montmartre and in the tonier parts of town. **MWC**

PLATE 31
Henri de Toulouse-Lautrec, *Troupe de Mademoiselle Eglantine* (Mademoiselle Eglantine's Troupe), 1896, color lithograph

Jane Avril commissioned this poster for her tour of England with Mademoiselle Eglantine's troupe. Avril is pictured at far left, slightly out of step with her dance partners. **MWC**

PLATE 32
Henri de Toulouse-Lautrec, *May Belfort*, 1895, color lithograph

Henri de Toulouse-Lautrec was enchanted with Irish chanteuse May Belfort, making several lithographs of her in 1895. In this, his only poster for Belfort, he focused on her glossy black ringlets, which rhyme with the sinuous tail of her little black cat. **MWC**

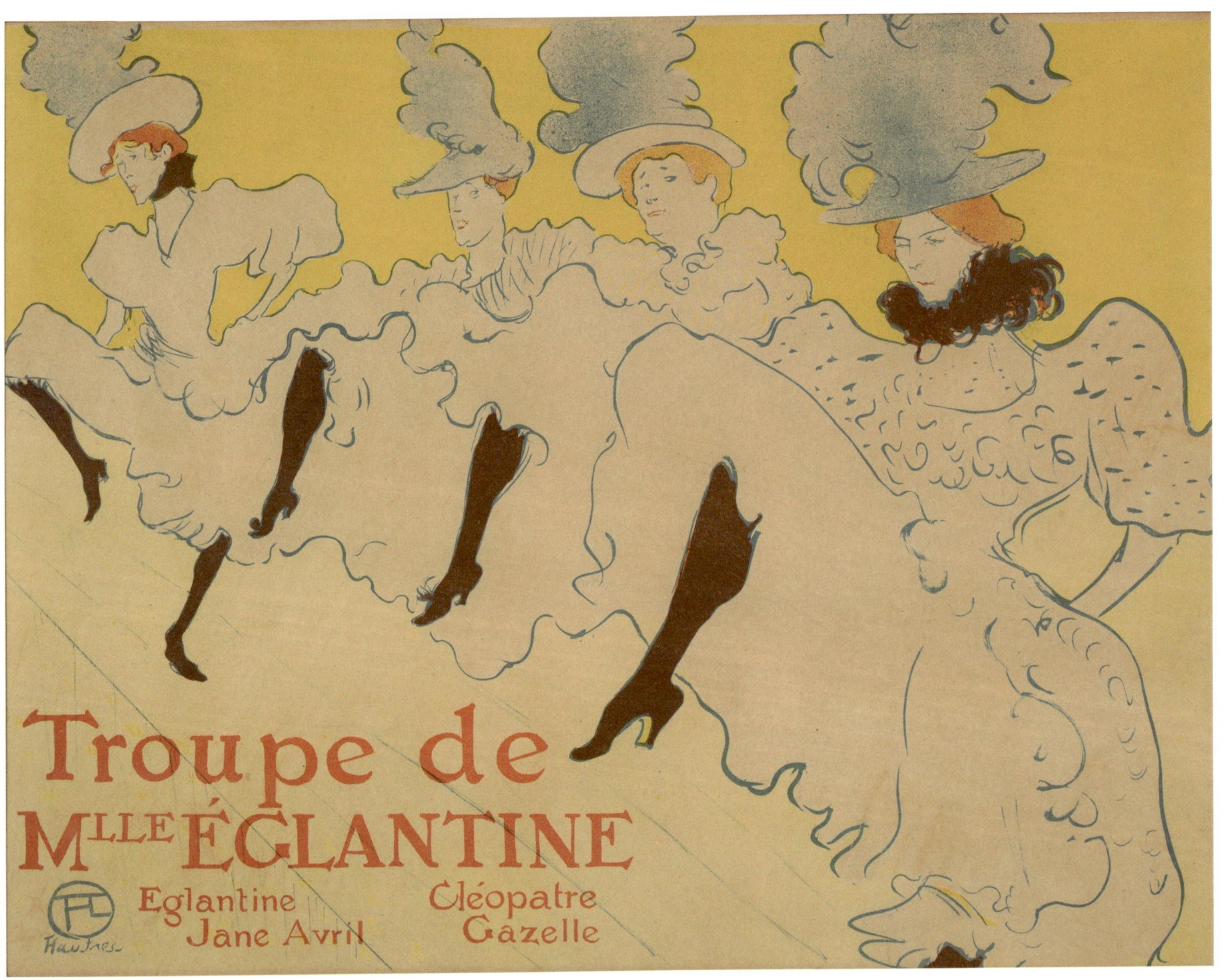

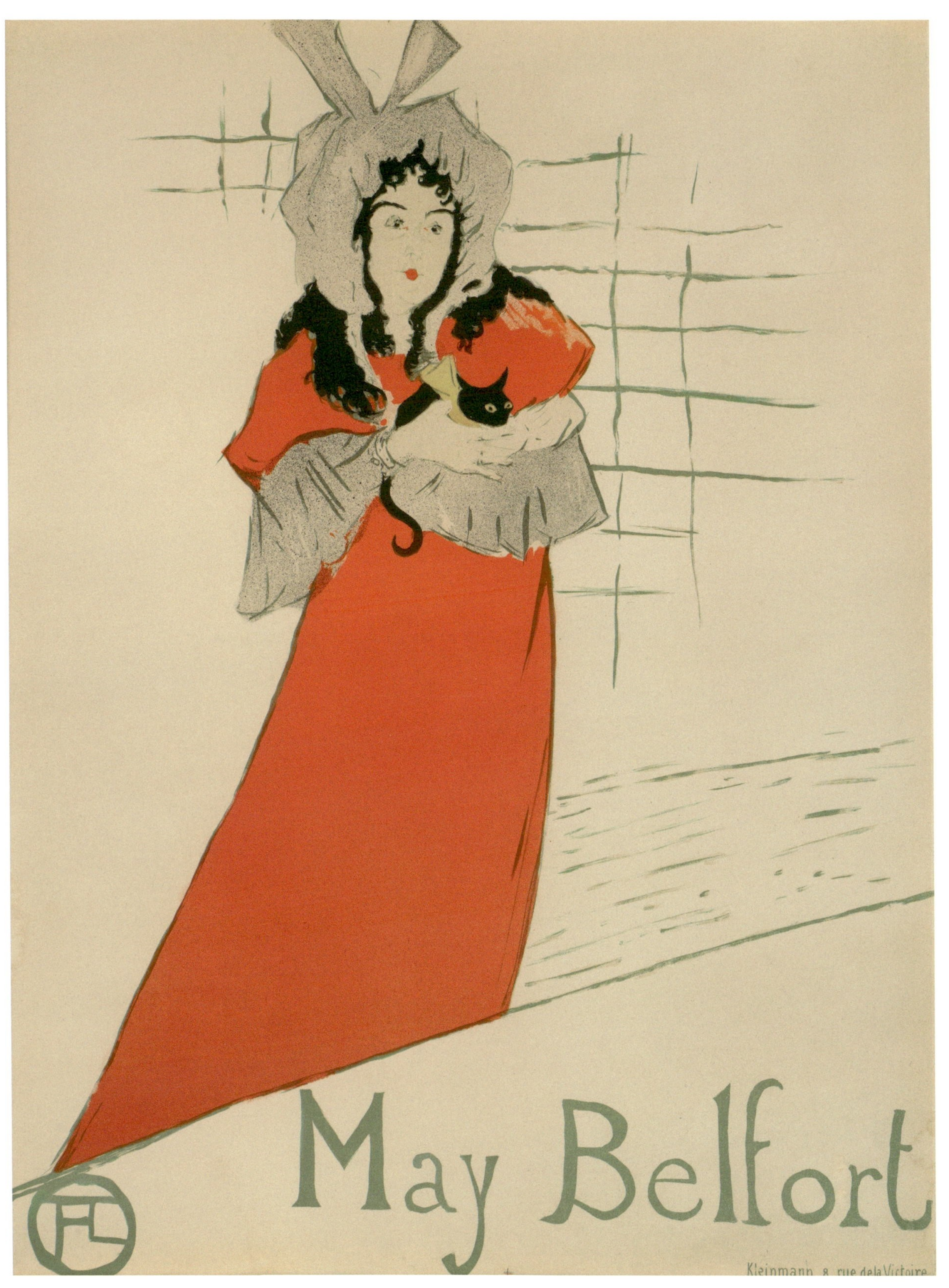

May Belfort
Kleinmann 8 rue de la Victoire

PLATE 33
Henri de Toulouse-Lautrec, *May Milton*, 1895,
color lithograph

For May Milton's tour of the United States,
Henri de Toulouse-Lautrec used five colors to
create this dynamic poster. Milton appears to
float across the floorboards in her voluminous
skirts. The calligraphic line of her hem and the
vermicular forms of her pink underskirts point
to Toulouse-Lautrec's appreciation of Japanesque arabesques. **MWC**

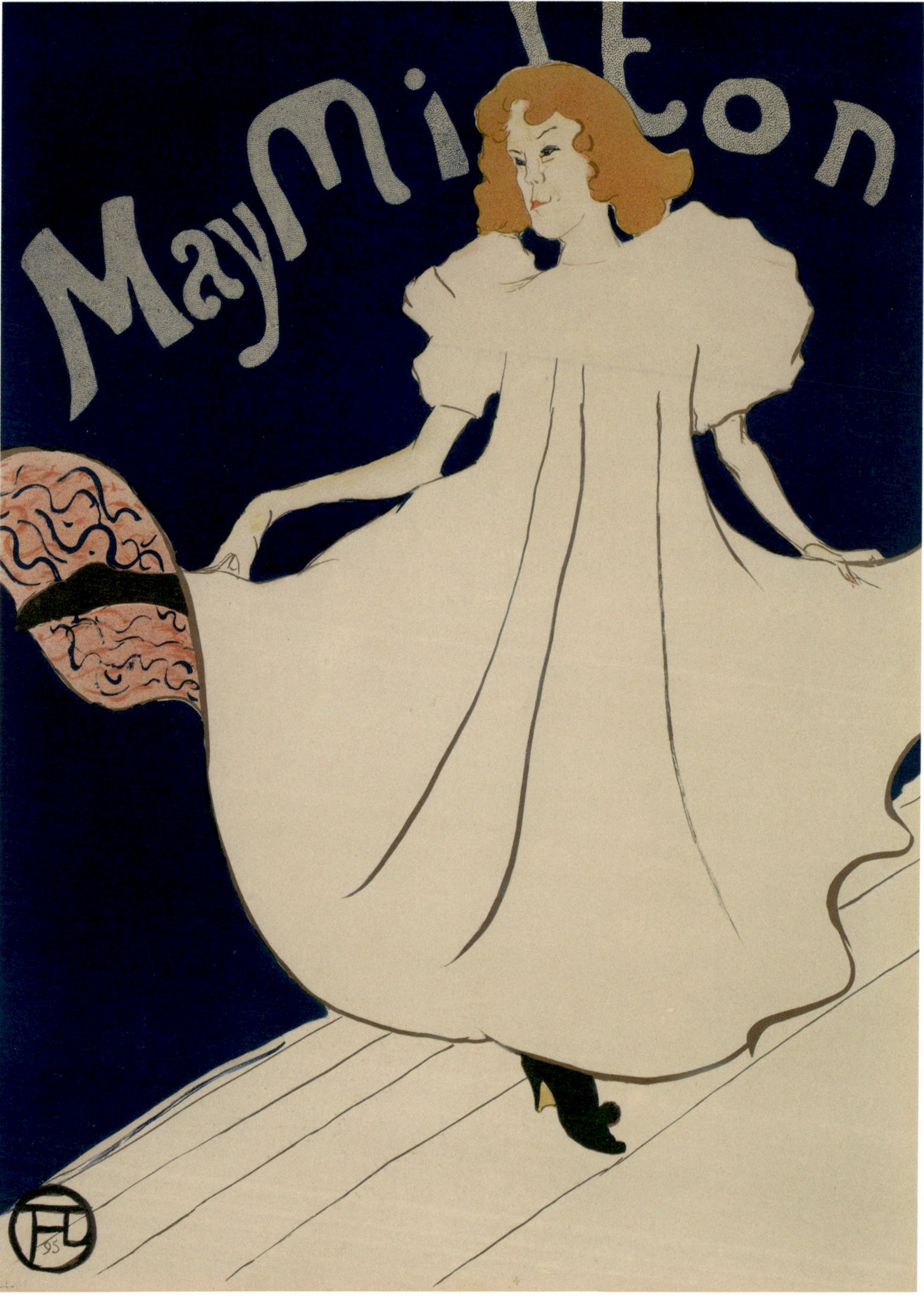

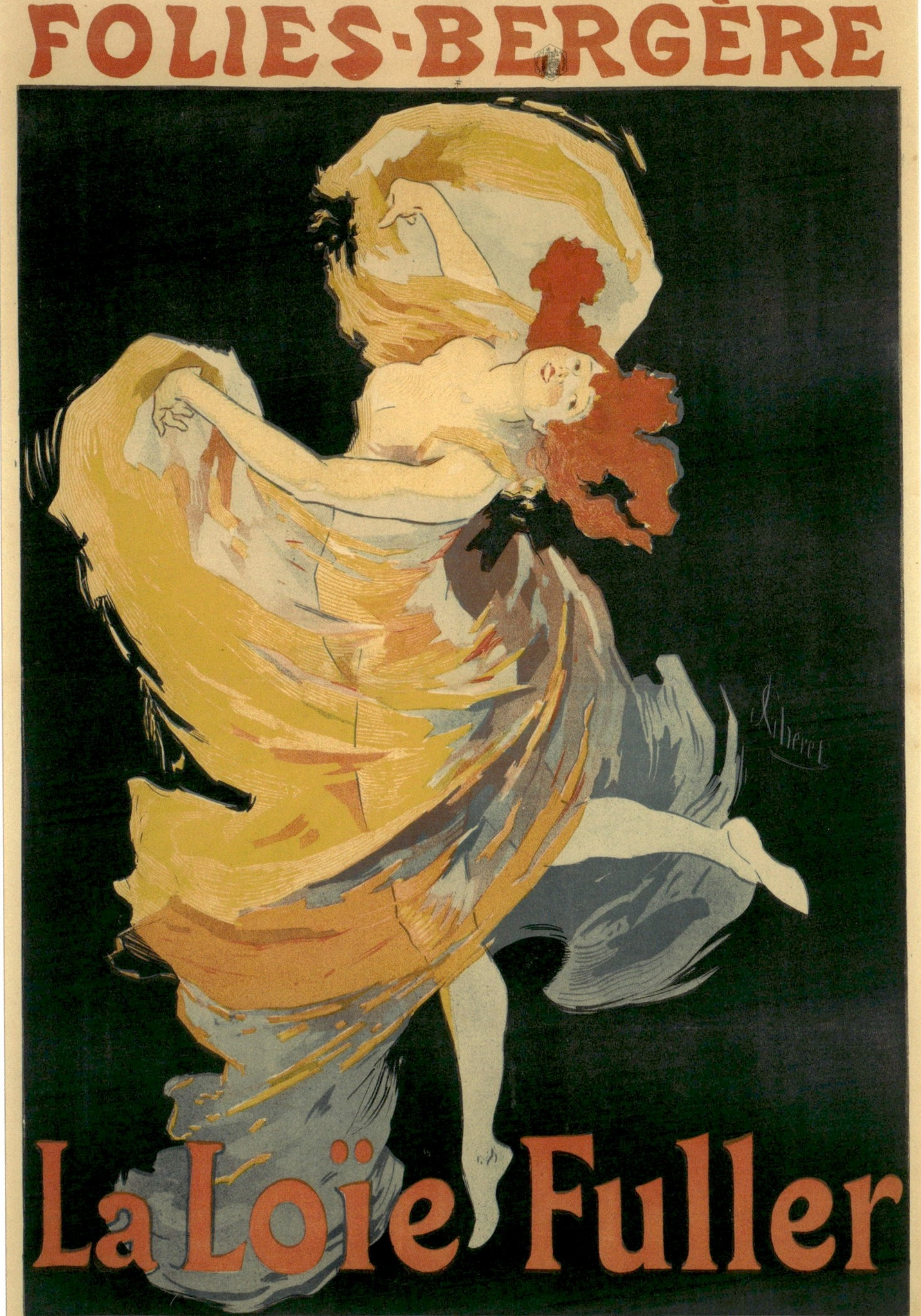

Jules Chéret, *Loïe Fuller*, 1893, color lithograph

American dancer Loïe Fuller made her name in Paris with her inventive performances. She surpassed the cliché of skirt dances by including moving lights, sound, and highly artistic choreography. She was among the most popular attractions in Paris, drawing both bohemian and bourgeois audiences. **MWC**

PLATE 35
Henri de Toulouse-Lautrec, *Aristide Bruant in His Cabaret*, 1893, color lithograph

Henri de Toulouse-Lautrec's bold depiction of Aristide Bruant in his dashing cape has often been compared to ukiyo-e actor portraits. The simplicity of the design and the masterful placement on the page make this one of the artist's most enduring posters. **MWC**

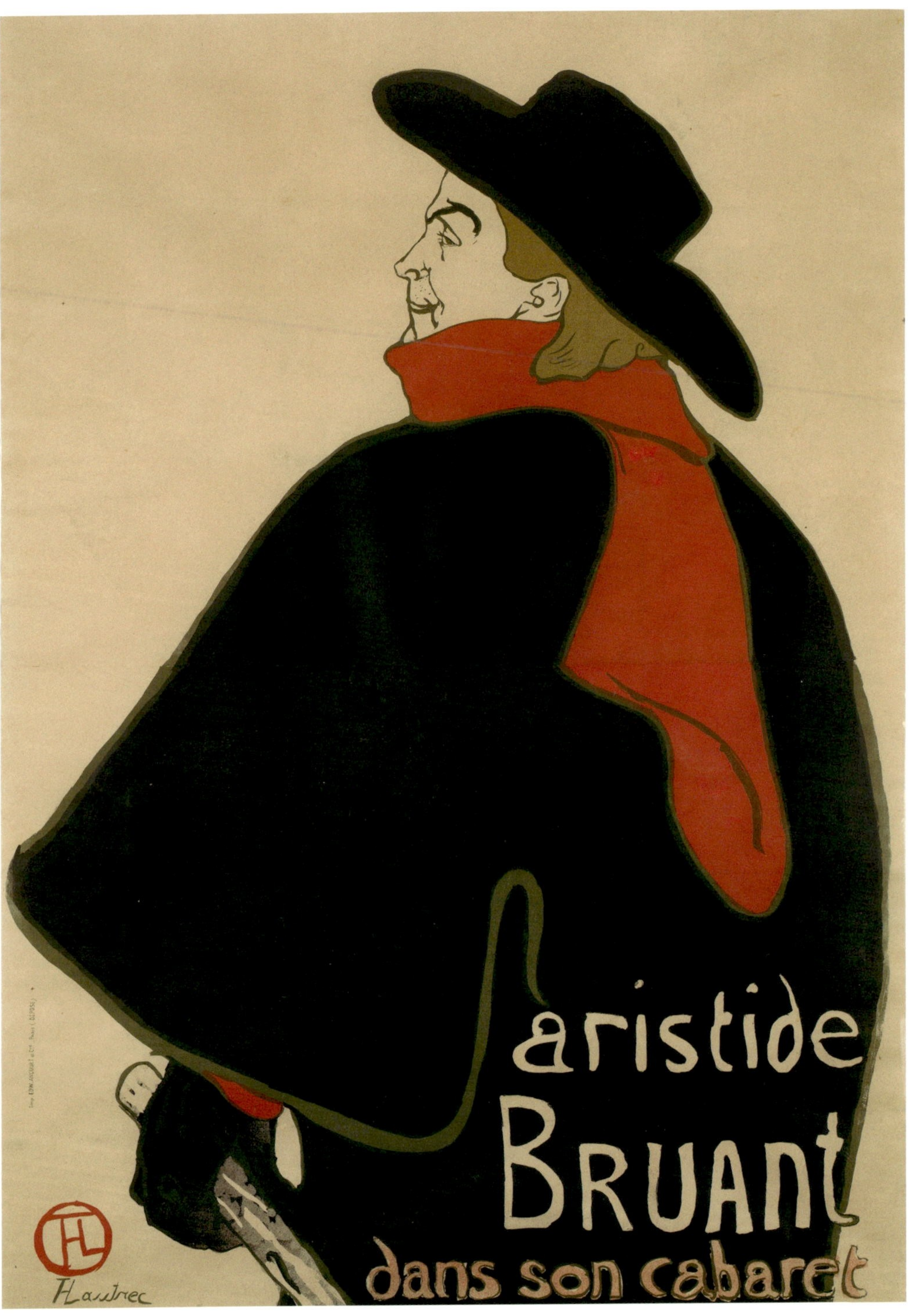

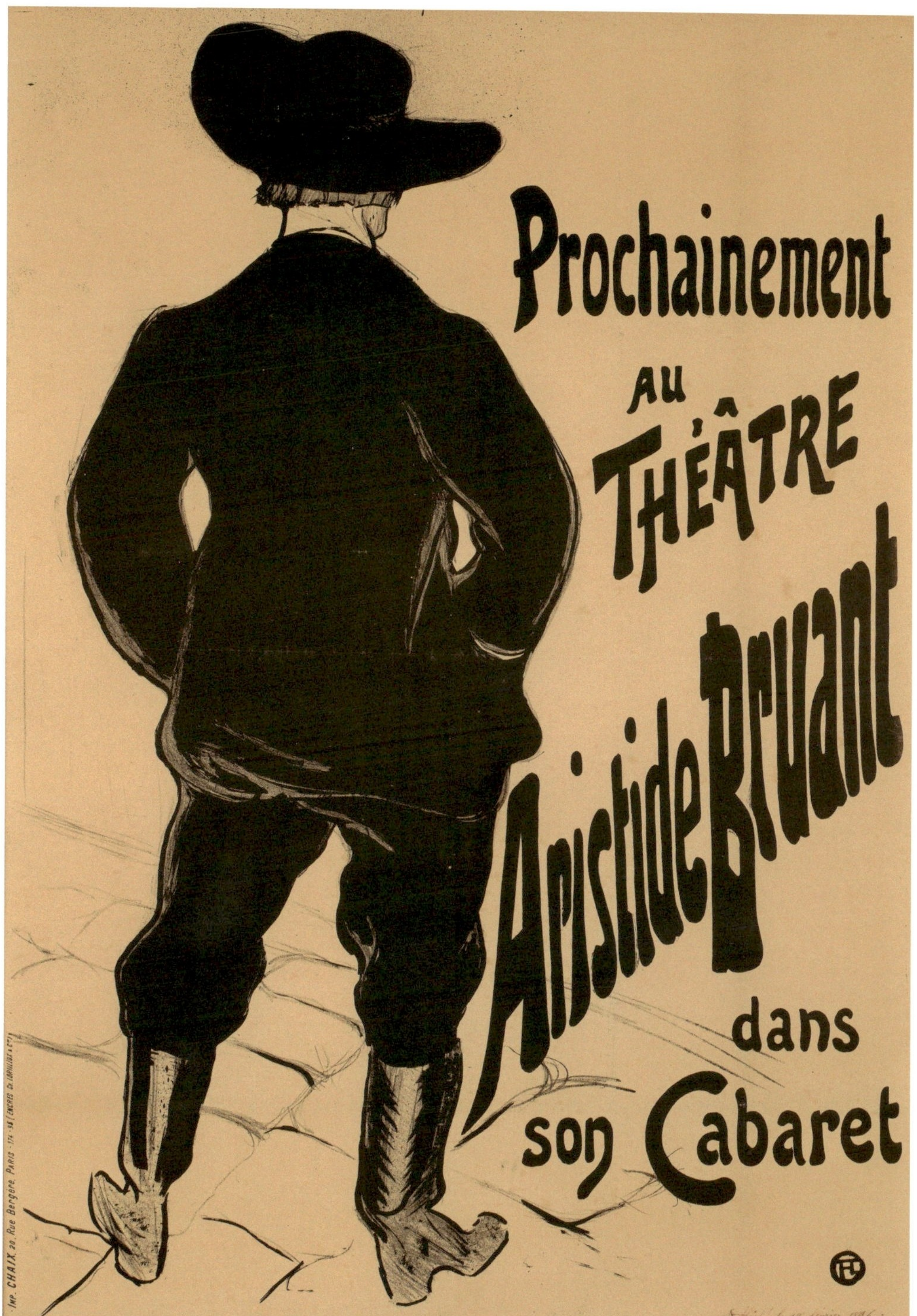

PLATE 36
Henri de Toulouse-Lautrec, *Aristide Bruant at the Mirliton*, 1893, lithograph

Aristide Bruant and his signature costume were so famous that passersby could even identify him from behind. Moreover, he was known for being playfully rude to his audiences. In this case, he literally turns his back on his adoring fans. **MWC**

PLATE 37
Henri de Toulouse-Lautrec, *Marcelle Lender*, 1895,
color lithograph

Henri de Toulouse-Lautrec's technically demand-
ing eight-color portrait of actress Marcelle Lender
shares compositional affinities with ukiyo-e depictions of courtesans, as does his prominent placement of his Japanesque monogram at the upper
left of the sheet. MWC

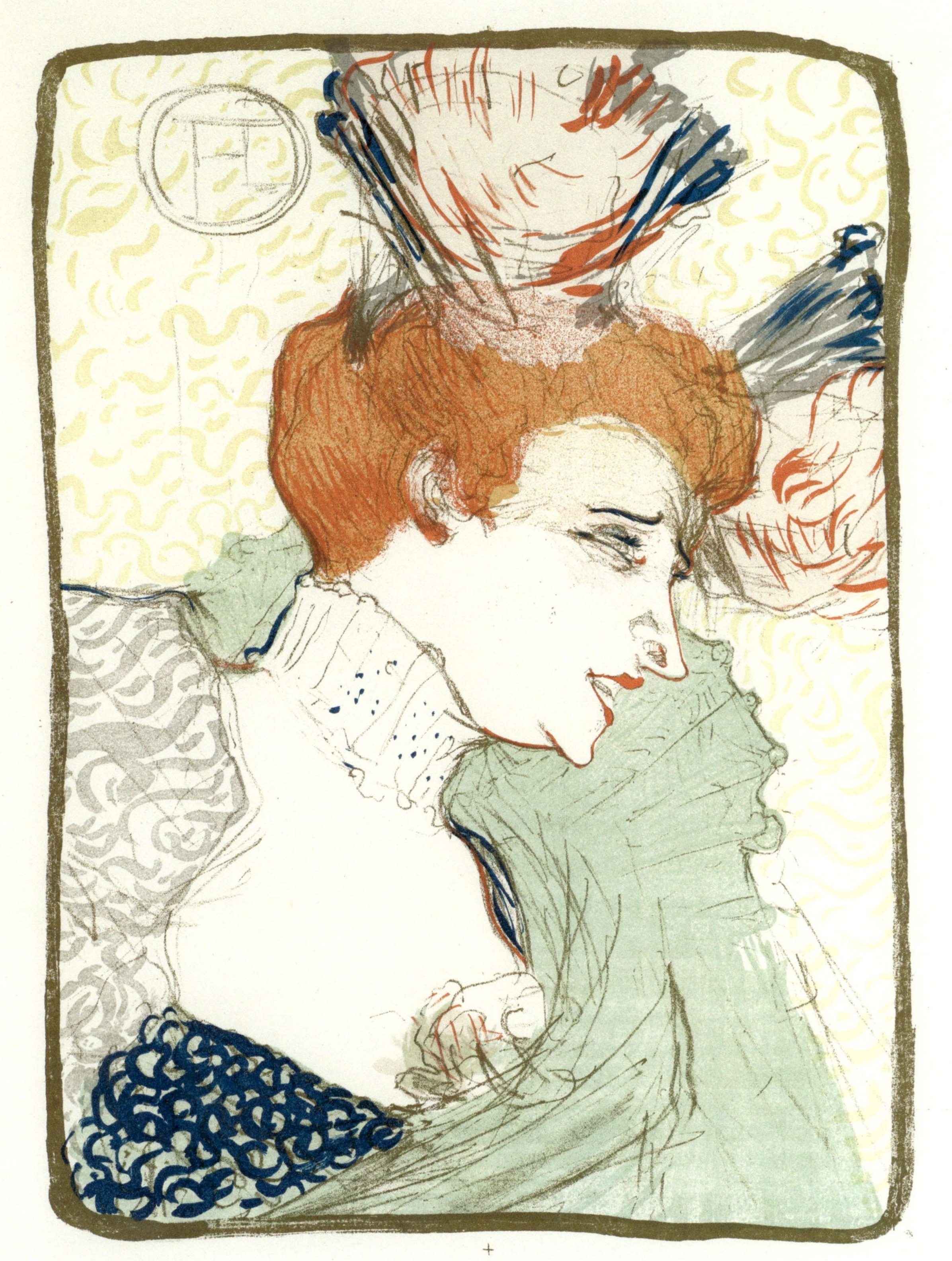

69/100

Pleasure Quarters

A large influx of samurai from different parts of the country came to Edo; that migration resulted in men outnumbering women by more than two to one, giving rise to a booming sex industry. The main licensed brothel district in Edo was Yoshiwara, an enclosed area with its boundaries clearly marked by walls and a moat. Only men were allowed to enter, through a single gate. After a night's revelry, they would leave at dawn, as depicted in a print by Utagawa Hiroshige (1797–1858) [38]. This five-block quarter was the main locale for worldly pleasures and fantasy in Edo for two centuries, from the mid-1600s until 1868, when the Meiji emperor assumed power and the city of Edo changed its name to Tokyo. Many people were employed to support the business. Based on accounts in various sources, an average of around three thousand women worked in the quarter at any given time.[1] More than by their physical features, the women in Yoshiwara were ranked by culturally constructed notions of beauty, which included accomplishments in music, dance, calligraphy, and even poetry. The highest-ranking were trendsetters in fashion and coiffure [42], and they were expected to be refined in etiquette [41]. It is important to recall that prints of "beautiful women" were idealized portrayals of sex work-ers;[2] commissioned by brothel owners, these prints functioned as marketing materials [39, 43]. Kitagawa Utamaro (1753–1806), a "connoisseur of women," was best known for his portrayals of women in the pleasure quarters.[3] His prints were results of col-laborations between the brothel owners, the publishers, and the artist; as such, they were essentially products of a commercial venture for Yoshiwara.[4]

Edmond de Goncourt (1822–1896), the French writer who penned the first monograph on Utamaro in 1891, intro-duced Utamaro's work to French audiences, including Henri de Toulouse-Lautrec (1864–1901). From the Goncourt brothers, Toulouse-Lautrec acquired a copy of Utamaro's notorious album of erotic prints, *The Poem of the Pillow*.[5] The brothels in Paris, like those in Yoshiwara, were licensed, but the prostitutes were not ranked, promoted, or educated. Toulouse-Lautrec's *Elles* series [49–53, 56] concentrates on intimate scenes from those Parisian prostitutes' daily lives, but instead of depicting their "beauty," *Elles* contains candid, unidealized images of unadorned bodies. One device he borrowed from Utamaro is the use of mirrors as a way of reflecting the figure's emotions [41, 51]. In 1903, only two years after Toulouse-Lautrec's death, French-German art historian and painter Erich Klossowski (1875–1949) lauded him as "the Utamaro of Montmartre" and described how the artist with "shameless curiosity . . . nails [his subjects] with unheard of mastery of analysis."[6] Indeed, even though Toulouse-Lautrec did not identify the women in his prints, he presented them with a remarkable degree of individuality and sensitivity.

One special genre of Japanese prints concerning sexual pleasure is *shunga*, or erotic pictures [47]. They were produced in large quantities and were an expected part of the work of many artists. Governed by different moral values than those in the West, all classes of Japanese society enjoyed *shunga* as a sort of fantasized sexual pleasure.[7] Printed *shunga* were illegal after 1722, but their production was rarely suppressed, and they were revived in the 1740s, though their output fluctuated over the fol-lowing decades. Toulouse-Lautrec produced a small number of erotic images, but only a few have survived. **XW**

NOTES

1. The 1680 guide to Yoshiwara notes there were 2,868 courtesans that year; in the 1787 *Sho-cho no itomaki*, the author Santō Kyōden com-ments that the courtesans were 2,500; and records of the nineteenth century indicate there were 3,000 courtesans. Cited in Asano Shūgō, "Courtesans, Geisha, and Male Prosti-tutes," in Morse, *Drama and Desire*, 41 and 47.

2. Davis, *Picturing the Floating World*, 76; *Utamaro*, 23.

3. Davis, *Utamaro*, 7.

4. Davis, *Utamaro*, 24.

5. Ives, *The Great Wave*, 93.

6. Klossowski, *Die Maler von Montmartre* (Berlin: J. Bard, [1903]), 52, cited in Castleman and Wittrock, *Henri de Toulouse-Lautrec*, 12.

7. Not all *shunga* depict scenes in the Yoshiwara pleasure quarters. Some *shunga* were rented out to city residents, and some were used by newlyweds. Timon Screech argues the pri-mary purpose for *shunga* was for solitary sex; see his *Sex and the Floating World*, 7–8.

PLATE 38
Utagawa Hiroshige, *Dawn at the Entrance to Yoshi-wara*, from the series *One Hundred Views of Famous Places in Edo*, 1857, woodblock print

This is number 38 from Utagawa Hiroshige's celebrated series *One Hundred Views of Famous Places in Edo*. At dawn, the guests are walking out of the Great Gate of Yoshiwara, the licensed brothel district. Lovers parting at this hour is a tradition often described in Japanese literature; here, Hiroshige turned it into a lyrical picture of the floating world. **XW**

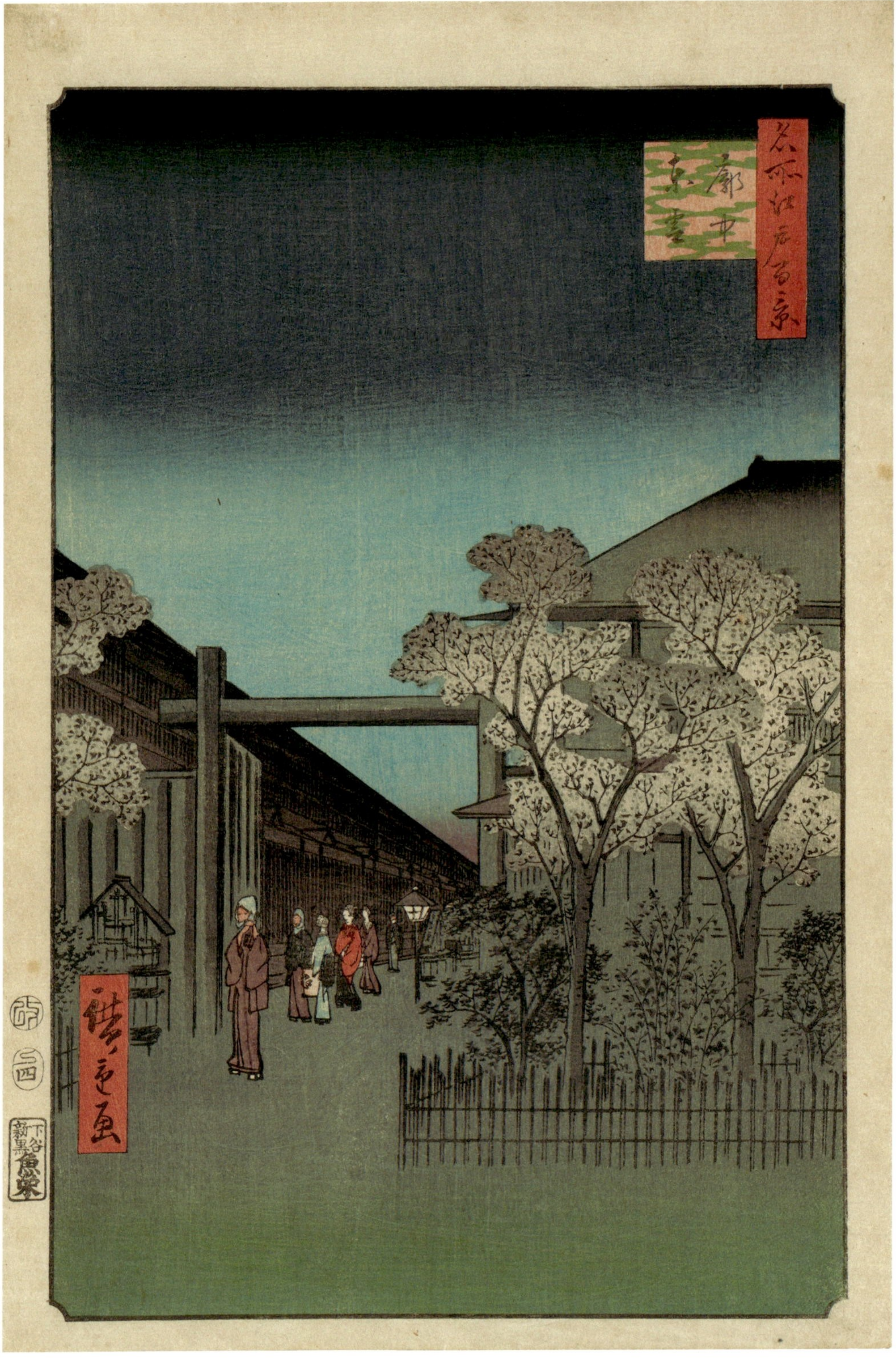

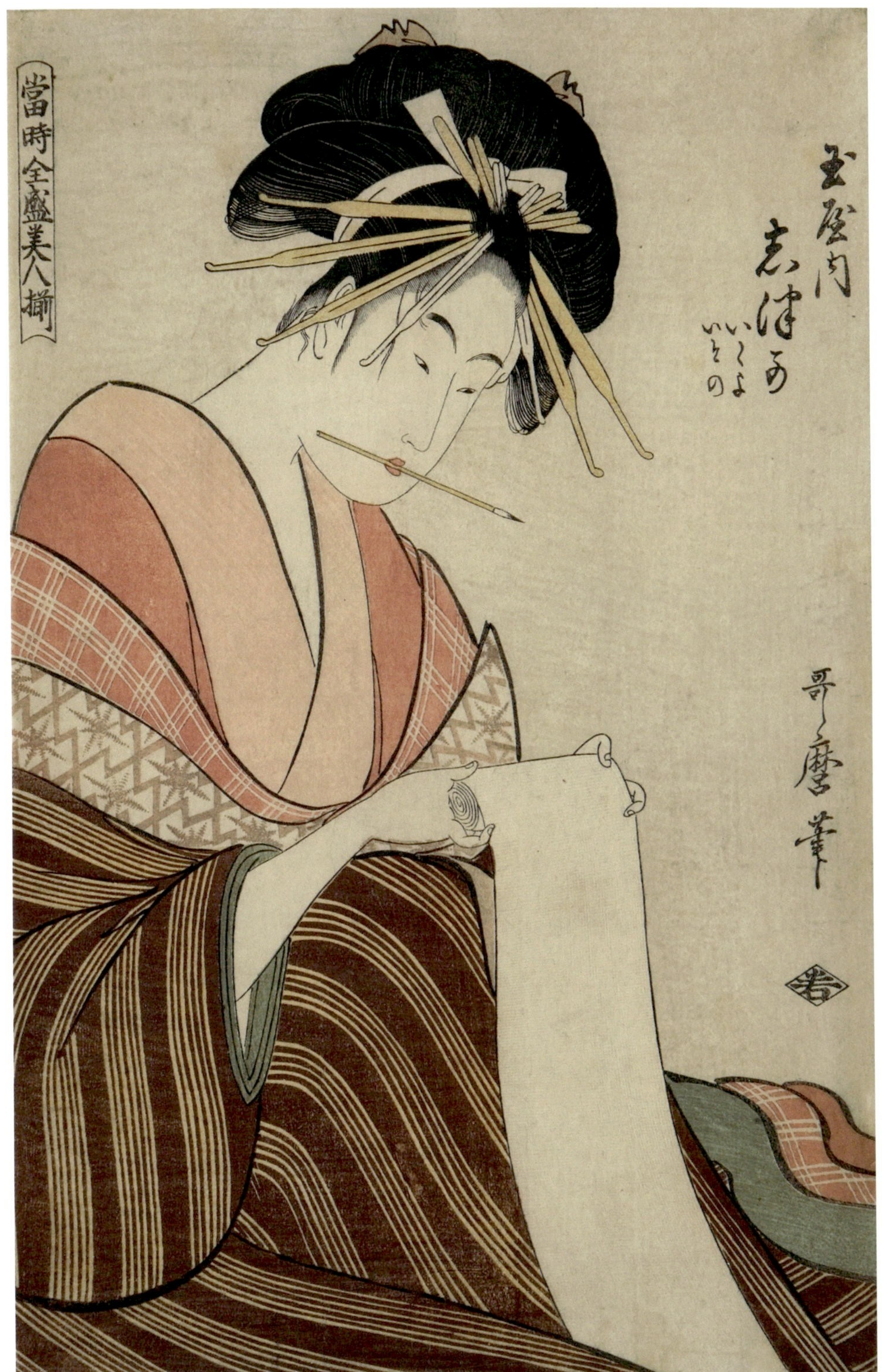

PLATE 39
Kitagawa Utamaro, *Shizuka of the Tamaya House*, from the series *A Complete Set of the Great Beauties of the Present Day*, 1794, woodblock print

This print depicts a high-ranking sex worker holding a brush between her teeth and rolling up a letter. The names of her attendants are written next to hers, confirming her status. The design was reworked from a previous one in which the sitter's thigh was revealed through her open kimono. As the composition changed, so did the name of the sitter, suggesting the portrait is not an image of a specific woman but of a general type. **XW**

PLATE 40
Kitagawa Utamaro, *Delivering a Letter*, from the
series *Elegant Five-Needled Pine*, 1797–98, woodblock print

A young maid is secretly slipping a letter into a
geisha's sleeve while whispering a message. This
print is from the series *Elegant Five-Needled Pine*,
which features five designs of pairs of figures
in half-length. The collar of the geisha's inner
kimono is coated with mica, adding a sparkling
touch. **XW**

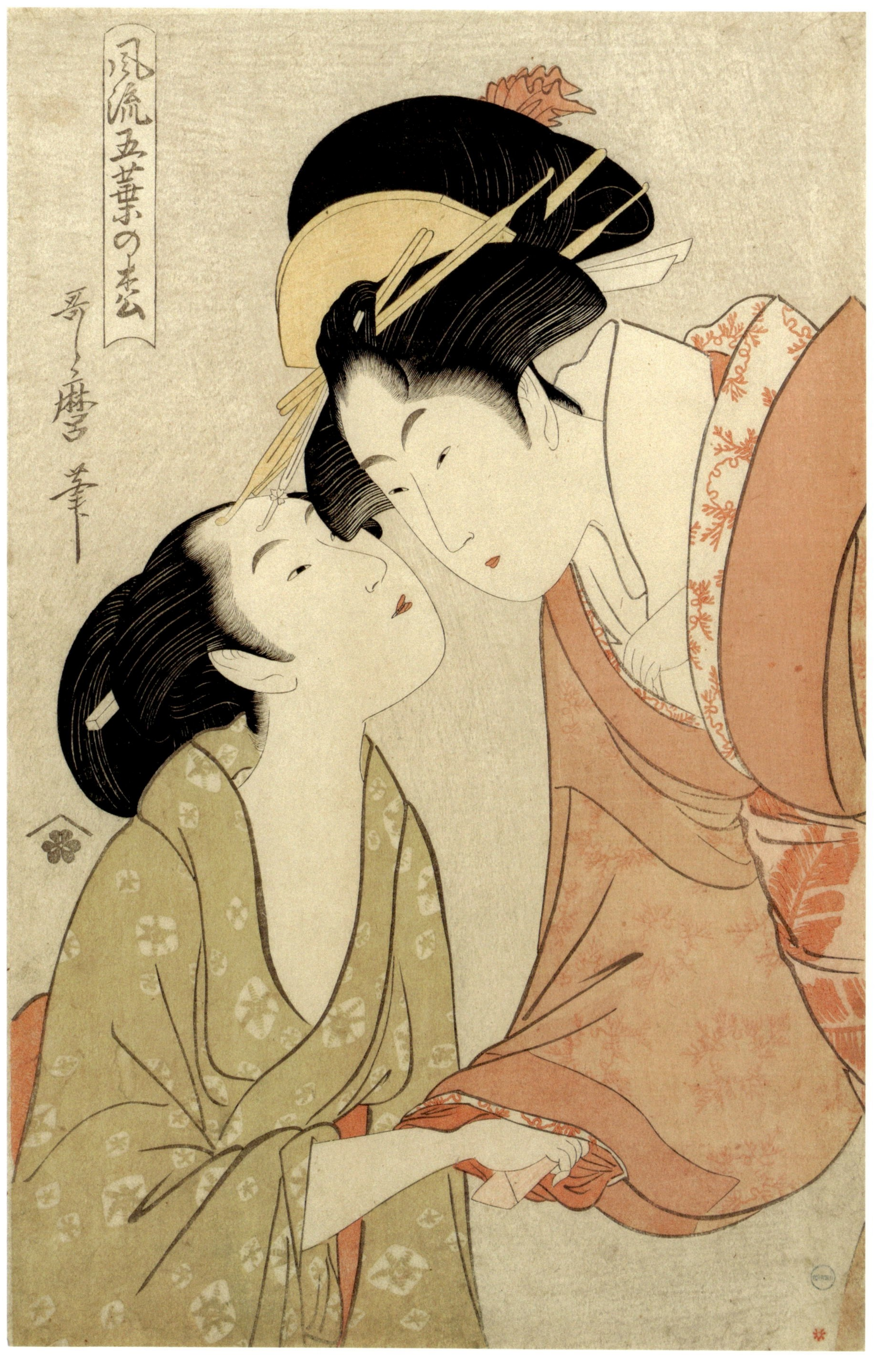
風流五葉の松
哥麿筆

PLATE 41
Kitagawa Utamaro, *Tagasode of the Tamaya House*,
1800–1802, woodblock print

The subject of this series is a parody of Ono no
Komachi, a celebrated ninth-century female poet
and a legendary beauty. The poem inscribed on
the print alludes to Komachi's literary talent. The
sitter here, Tagasode of the Tamaya brothel, is
gazing into a mirror. Her kimono and coiffeur suggest her high status, which is further confirmed
by the inclusion of her attendants' names in the
inscription. **XW**

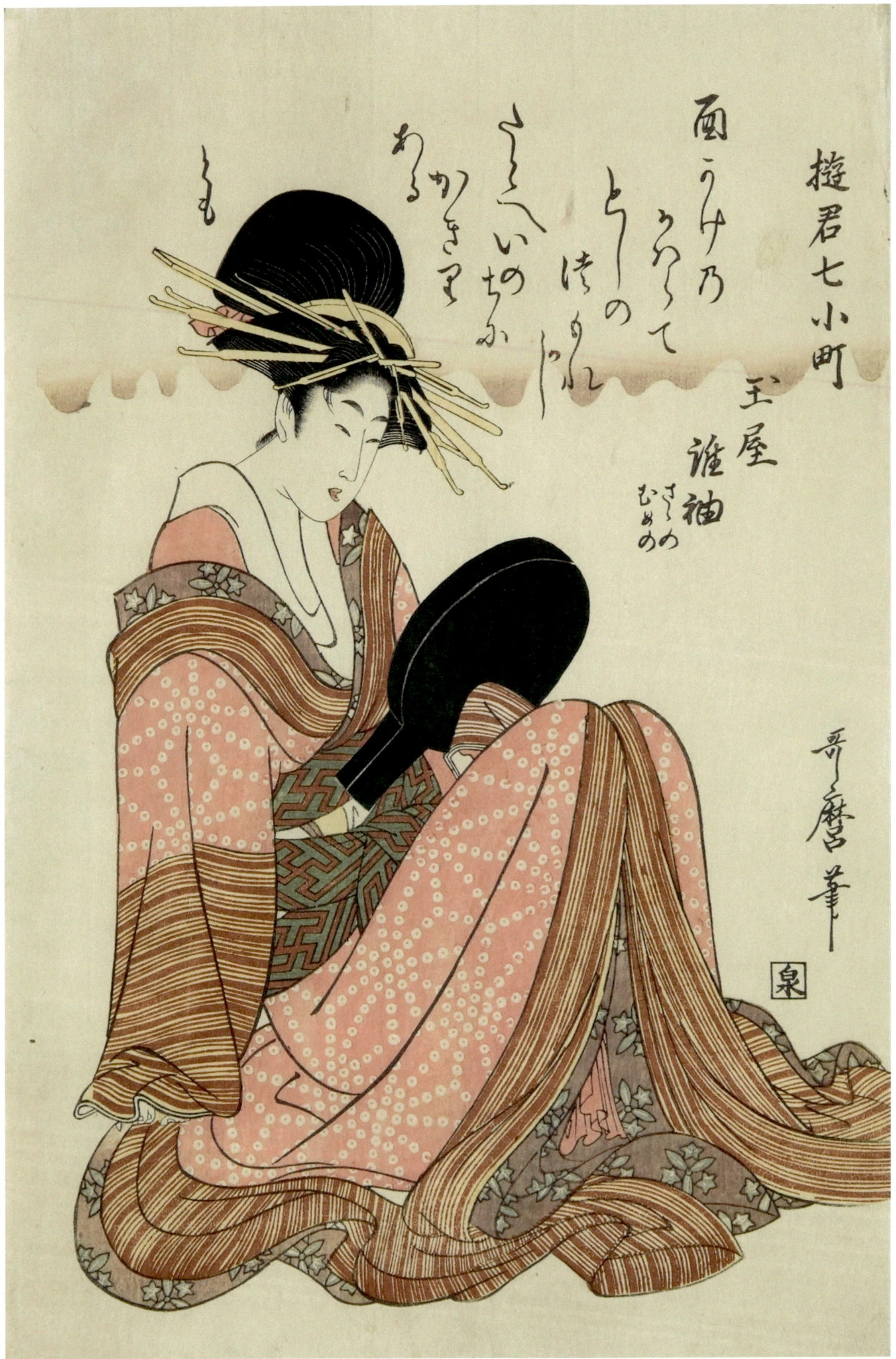

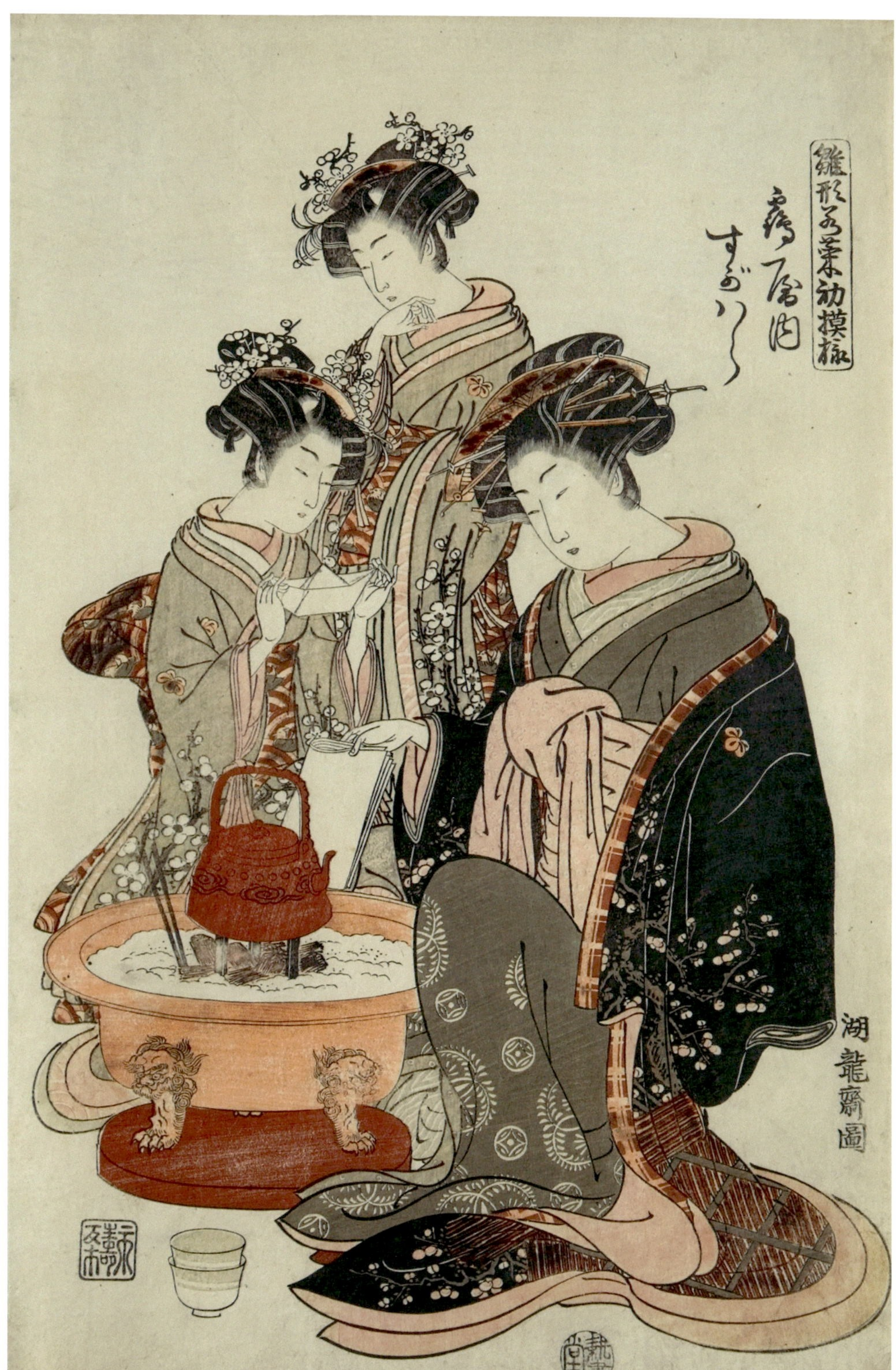

PLATE 42
Isoda Koryūsai, *Sugawara of the Tsuruya House with Two Attendants*, from the series *Models for Fashion*, ca. 1775, woodblock print

The *Models for Fashion* series was such a commercial success that its publication extended over five years, producing at least 140 designs. The prints were clearly promotional materials for the brothels as well as kimono merchants. Here, Sugawara of the Tsuruya brothel is dressed in the latest fashion, alongside her two attendants. **XW**

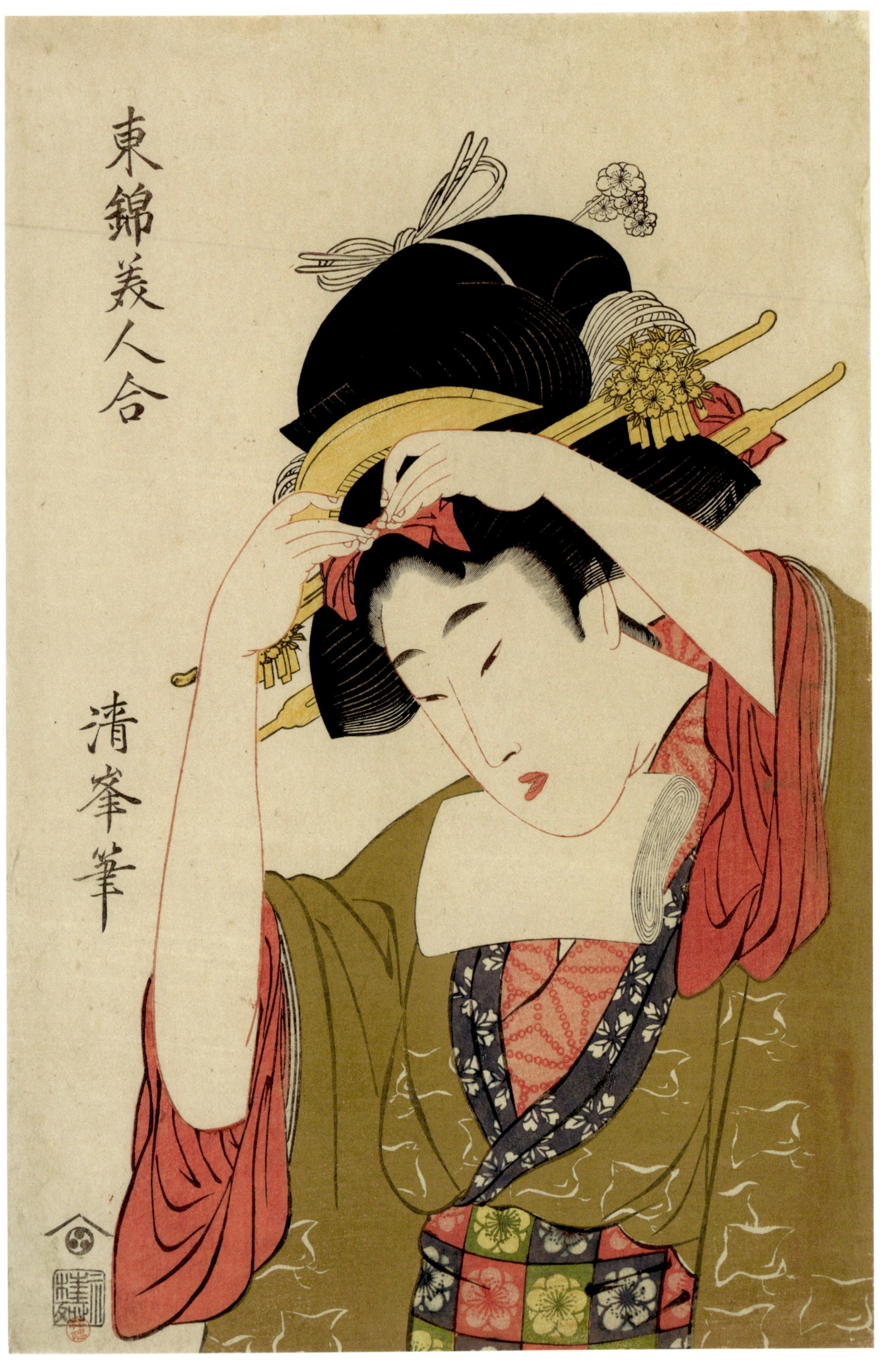
東錦美人合
清峯筆

PLATE 43
Torii Kiyomine, *A Beauty of the Eastern Brocade*,
ca. 1804–10, woodblock print

Torii Kiyomine designed a series of prints that
depict the beauties of Edo, many centered on the
daily life of sex workers in pleasure quarters. Here,
the woman lowers her head to adjust her hair, having tucked a roll of paper under her chin. **XW**

PLATE 44
Utagawa Toyokuni, *The Much-Frequented Komachi (Kayoi Komachi)*, ca. 1795, woodblock print

This print parodies a popular story drawn from a tragic Noh play. Here, a woman is returning from visiting her favorite customer, knowing that their meetings will eventually end. Utagawa Toyokuni sprayed ink to render the mist in the dark; this was a technique Henri de Toulouse-Lautrec adapted for his work, such as the cover for *Elles*. **XW**

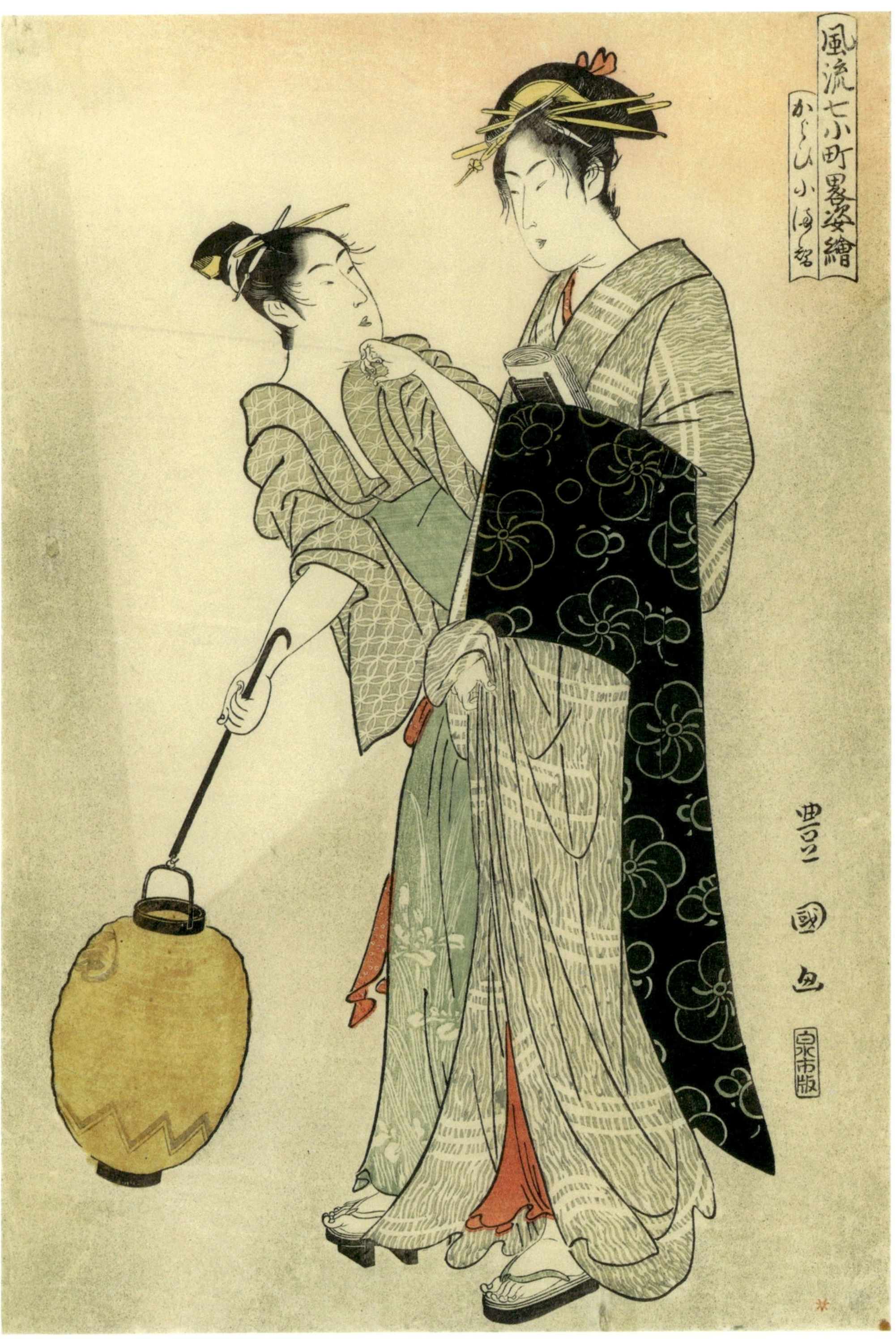

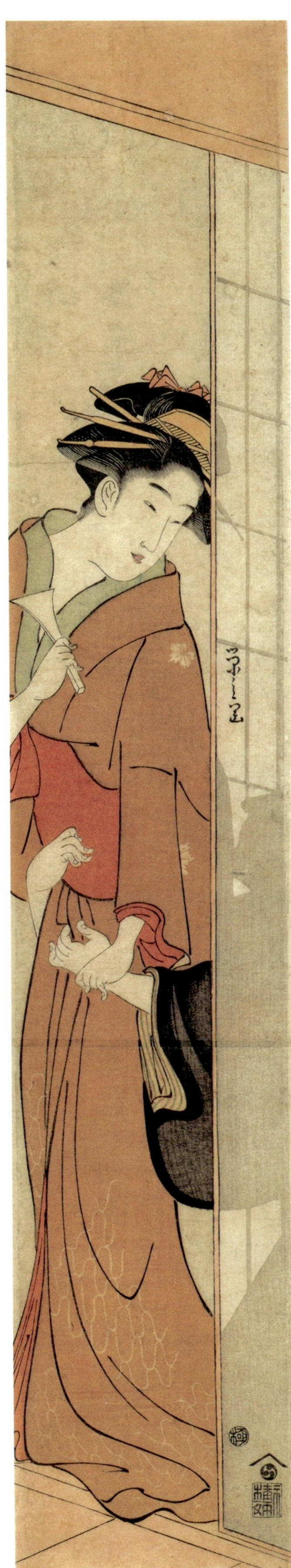

PLATE 45
Keisen Eishi, *A Geisha Wards off Unwanted Attention*, ca. 1795, woodblock print

In this "pillar-print" (a long, narrow format), a woman wards off a man who is reaching out his hand from behind the sliding door. The plectrum in her right hand indicates she plays the shamisen (a three-stringed instrument) and is hence a geisha, who was supposed to provide entertainment—singing, dancing, playing music, and having witty conversation—but not sexual service. **XW**

PLATE 46
Torii Kiyonobu I, *A Young Girl with Her Client*,
ca. 1710s, woodblock print

This monochrome print is an early, nonexplicit
example of *shunga*, or erotic pictures. Almost all
major print artists of the eighteenth and nineteenth centuries designed *shunga*, which were
consumed by people across the social classes.
The couple's bare feet and the girl's bashful look
render a rather suggestively erotic picture. **XW**

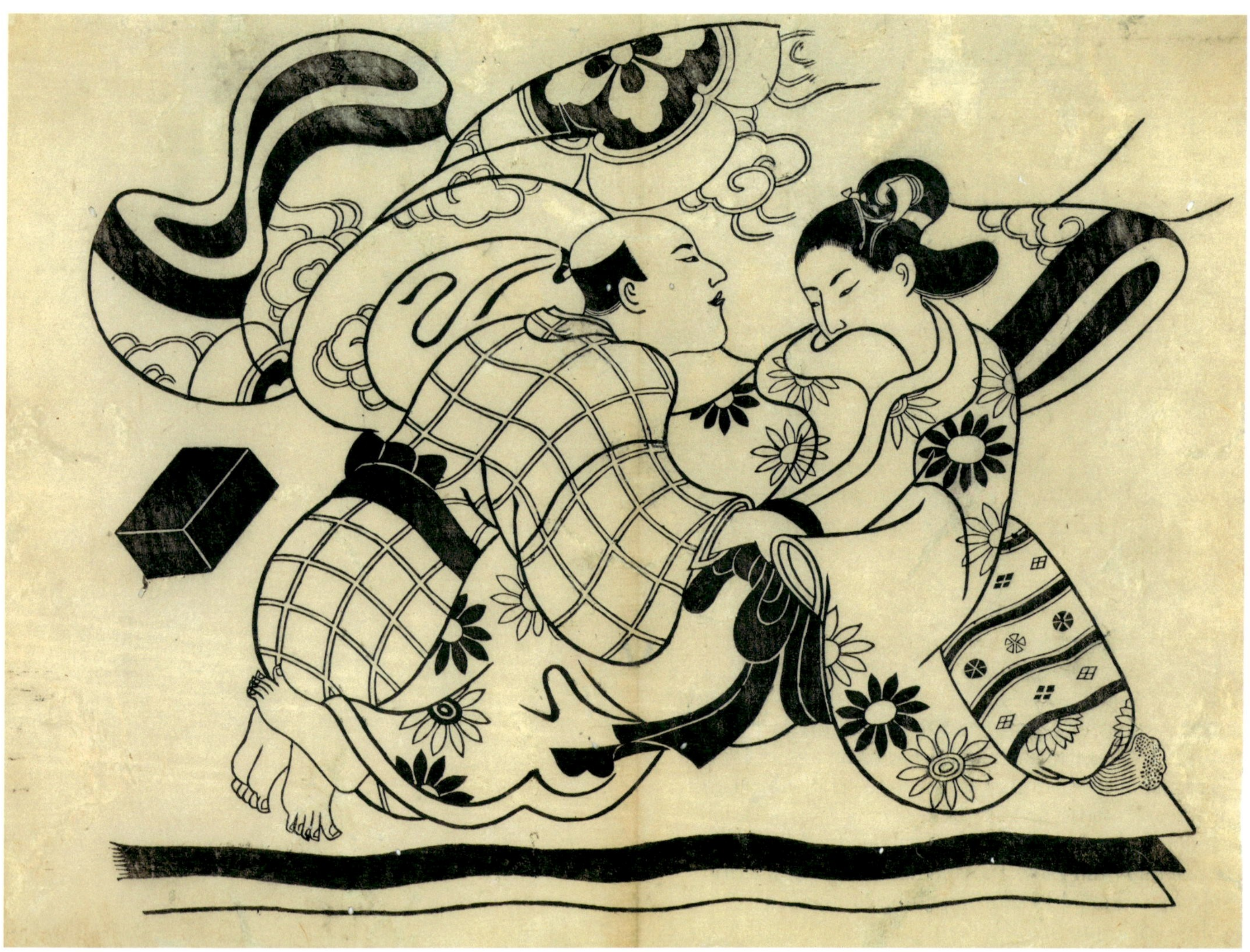

Kitagawa Utamaro, *A High-Ranking Yūjo with a Client*, 1799, woodblock print

This is a prefatory illustration for an album of erotic prints. While the other twelve prints depict explicit sexual encounters, this intimate scene portrays a high-ranking *yūjo* (sex worker; literally, "play woman"), judging from her elaborate coiffeur, alongside a recumbent young client who is smoking a tobacco pipe. **XW**

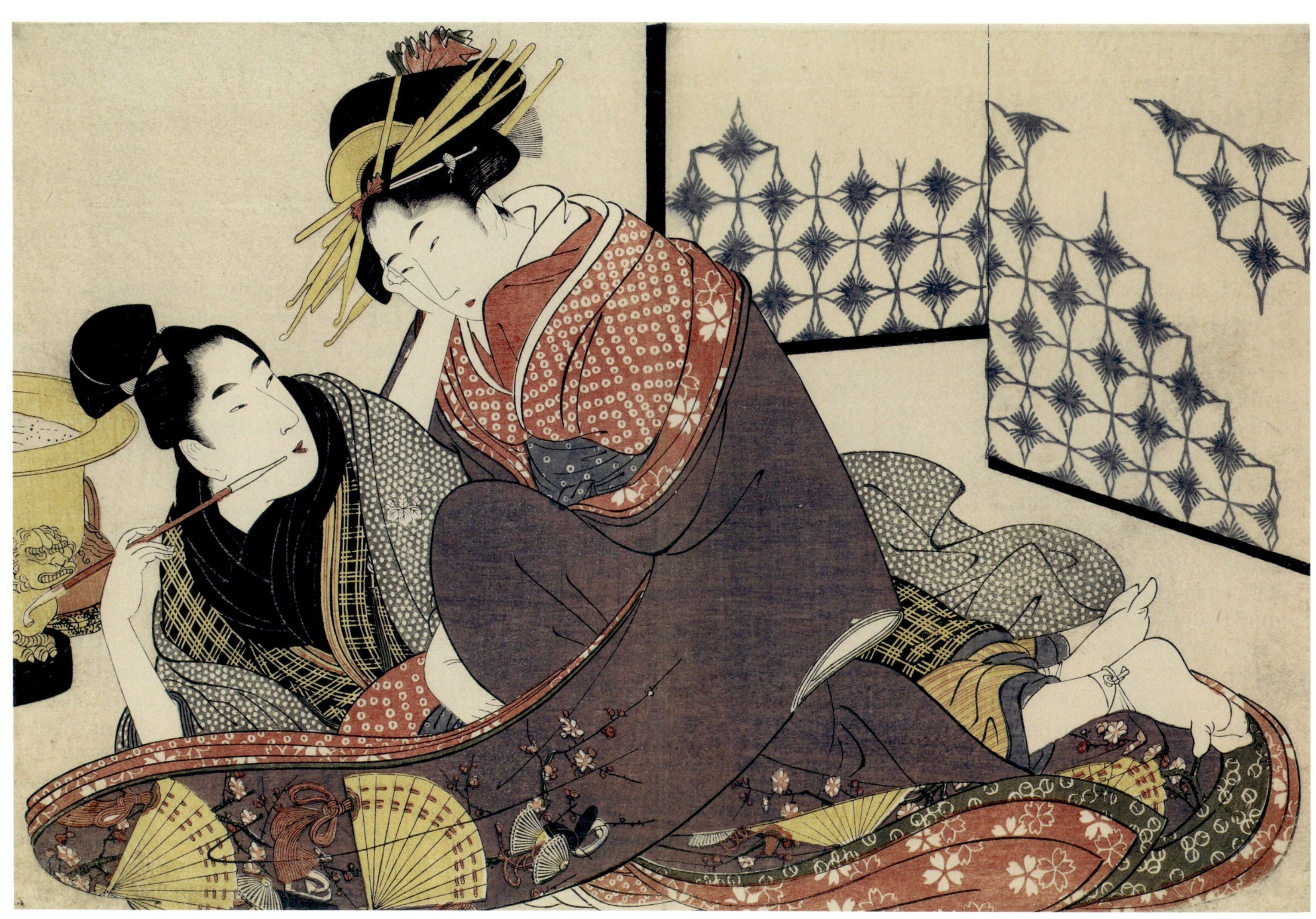

PLATE 48
Kitagawa Utamaro, *Needlework*, from the *Untitled Series of Scenes of Everyday Life*, ca. 1797–98, woodblock print

From a series of five prints that depict scenes of everyday life, this design shows a woman doing needlework. Her breasts are revealed through the translucent gauze, under which the cat has gotten caught. The veillike fabric evokes, though suggestively, a sense of eroticism. **XW**

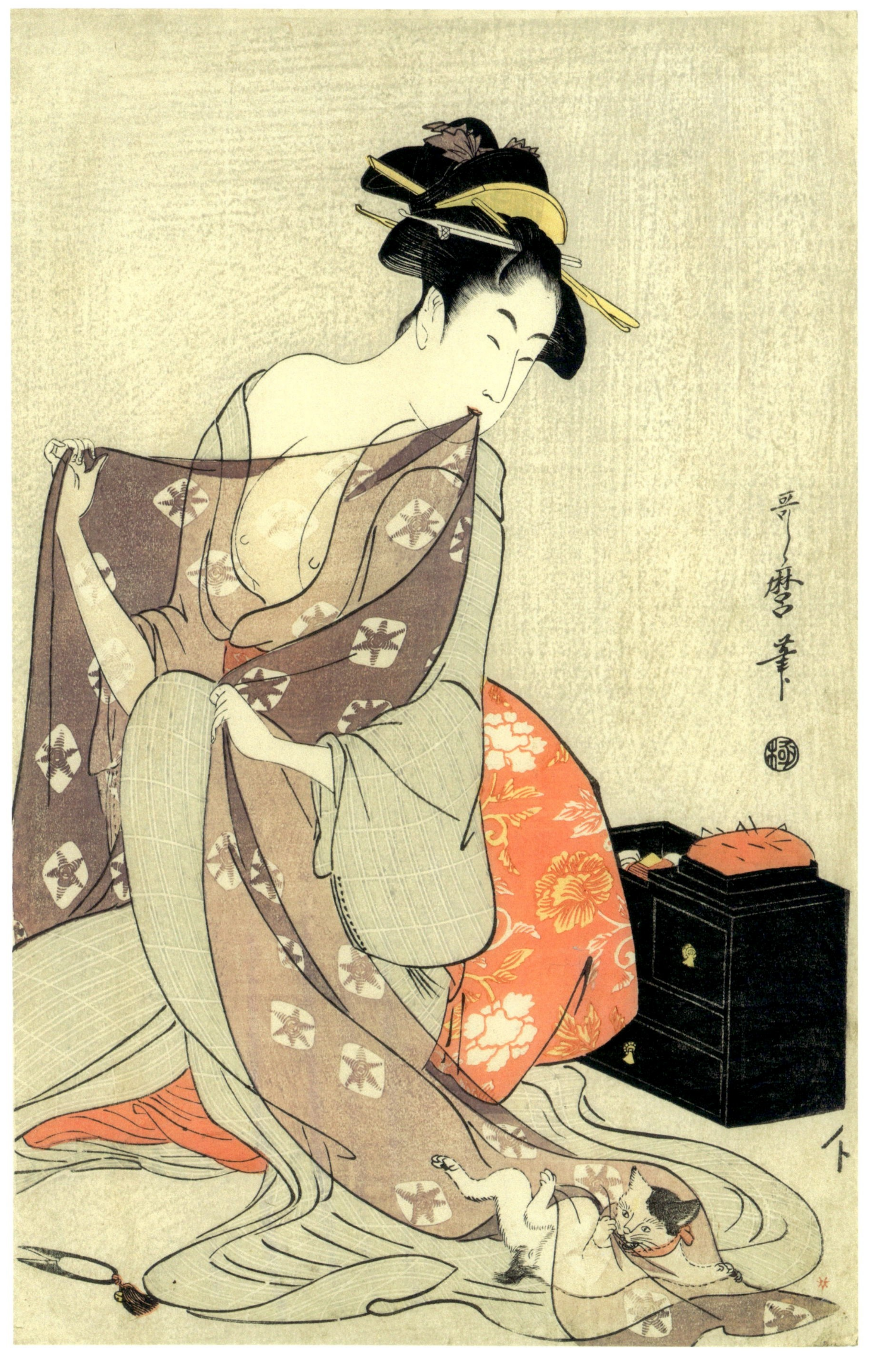

PLATE 49
Henri de Toulouse-Lautrec, Cover for the album
Elles, 1896, color lithograph

Henri de Toulouse-Lautrec's *Elles* is a suite of
twelve lithographs depicting daily life in a brothel.
The artist eschewed lascivious or titillating views,
focusing instead on the boredom and the rou-
tine chores of the women. Although unnamed
in the titles, many of the women are identifiable
from the sensitive graphite drawings that the artist made during his many visits to this *maison close*
(brothel). **MWC**

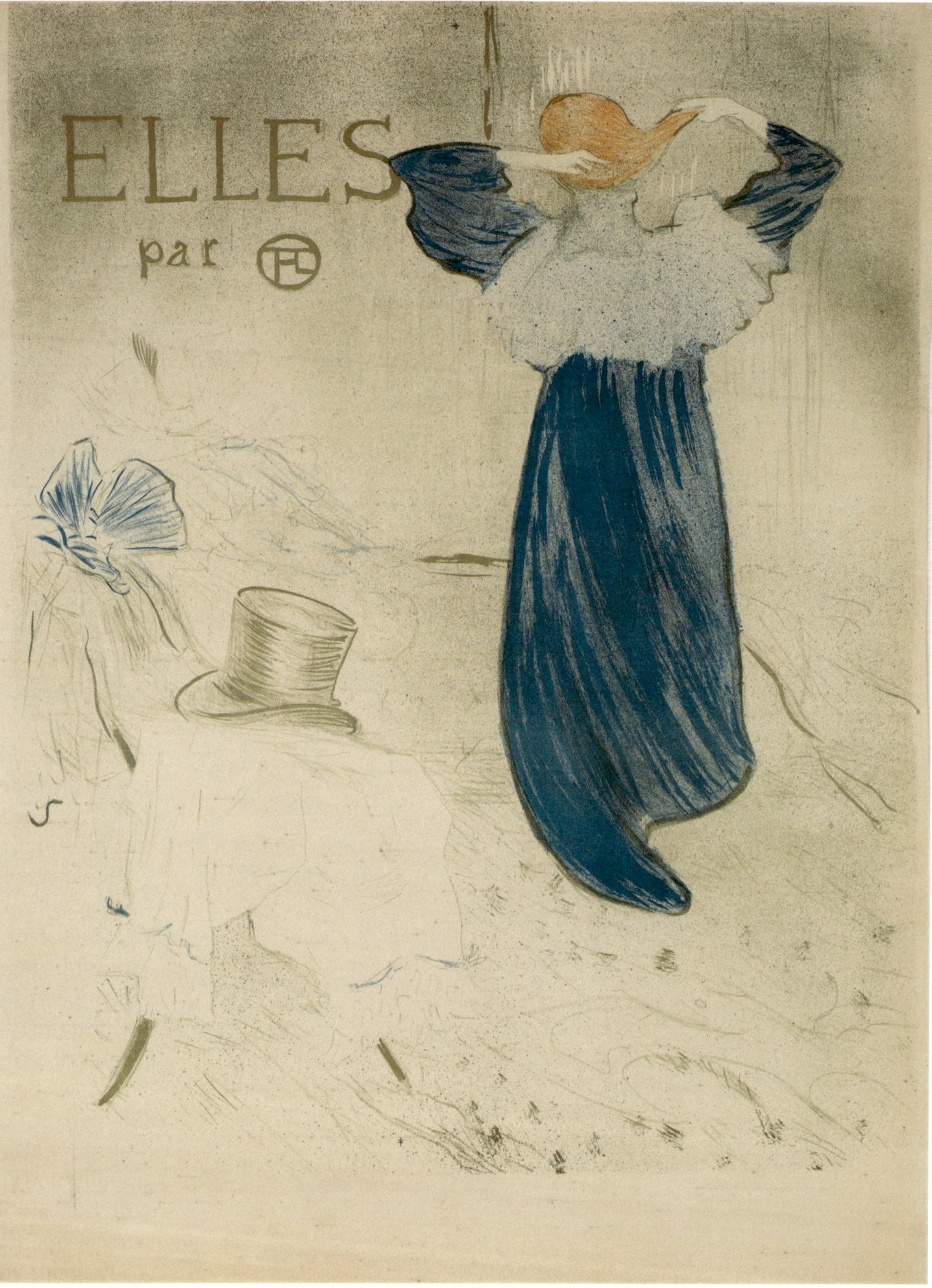

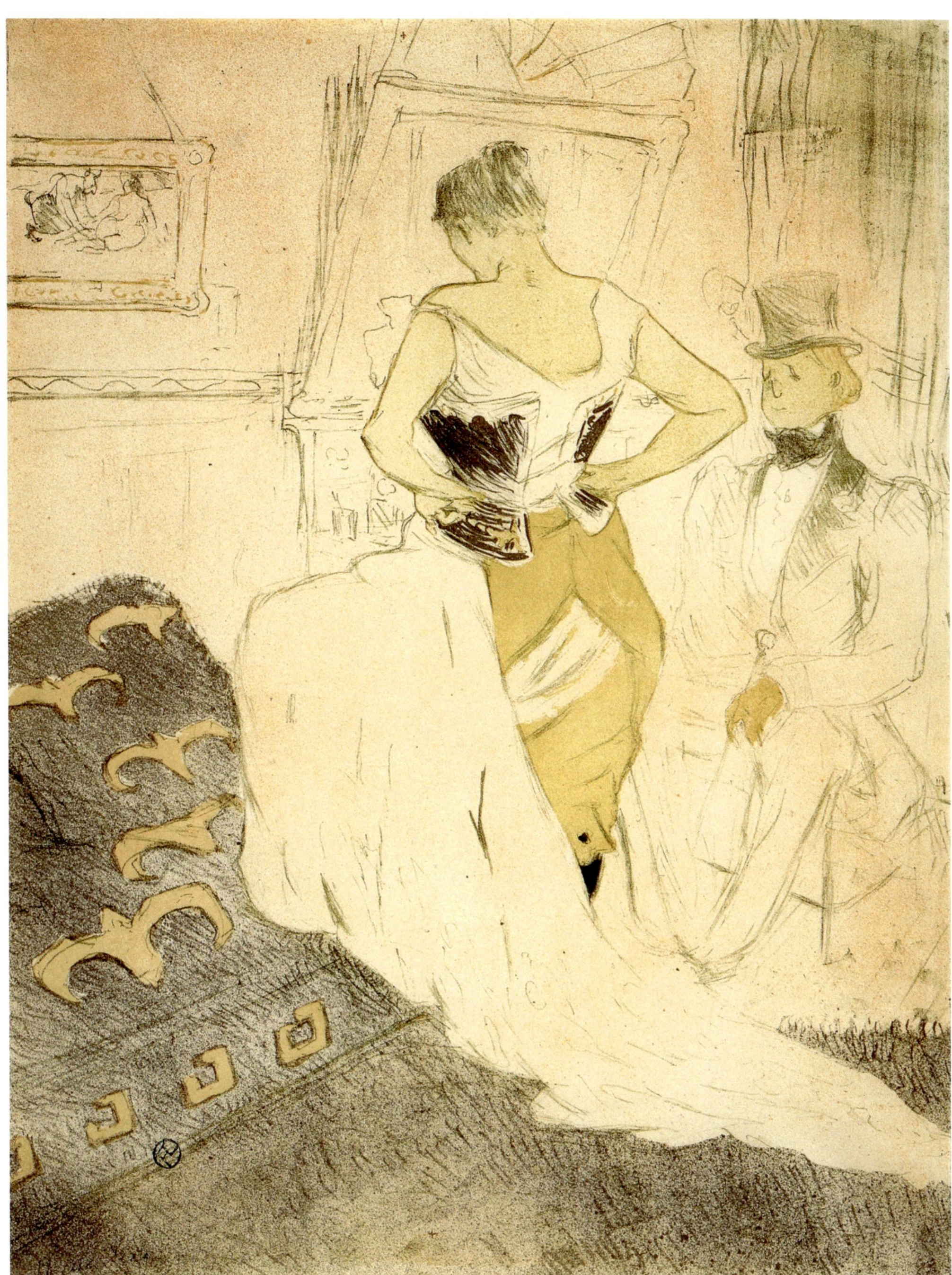

Henri de Toulouse-Lautrec, *Woman in a Corset*, from the album *Elles*, 1896, color lithograph

Henri de Toulouse-Lautrec transforms the erotic act of disrobing into another daily chore in this lithograph, the only sheet in *Elles* that includes a male figure with a prostitute. **MWC**

PLATE 51
Henri de Toulouse-Lautrec, *Woman with Hand Mirror*, from the album *Elles*, 1896, color lithograph

The motif of a woman with a mirror—common in both Japanese and French art—is often used to offer a second view of the beauty of the woman. Henri de Toulouse-Lautrec subverts this trope by denying the spectator the reflection and by depicting a rather plain, uneroticized woman. **MWC**

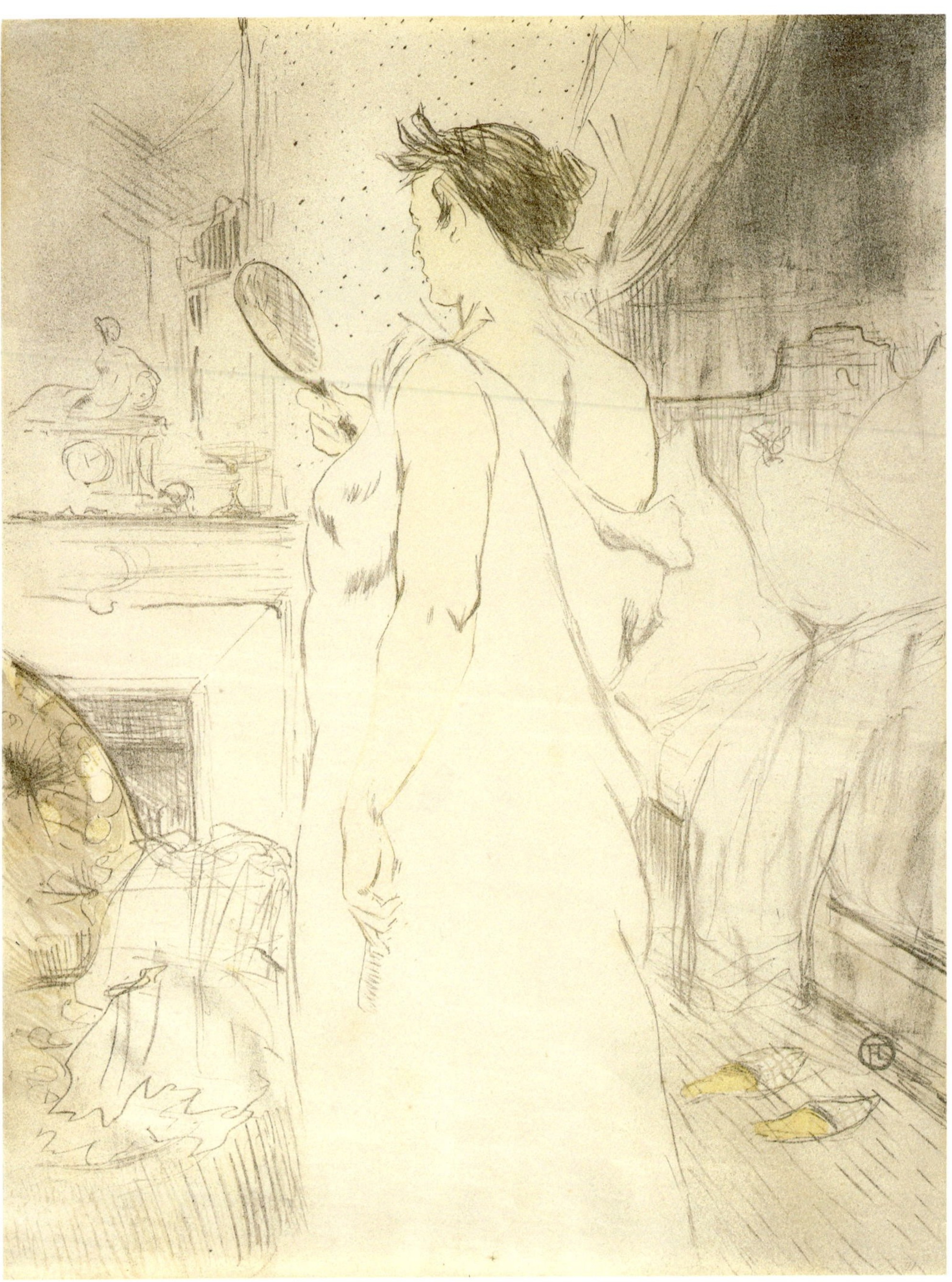

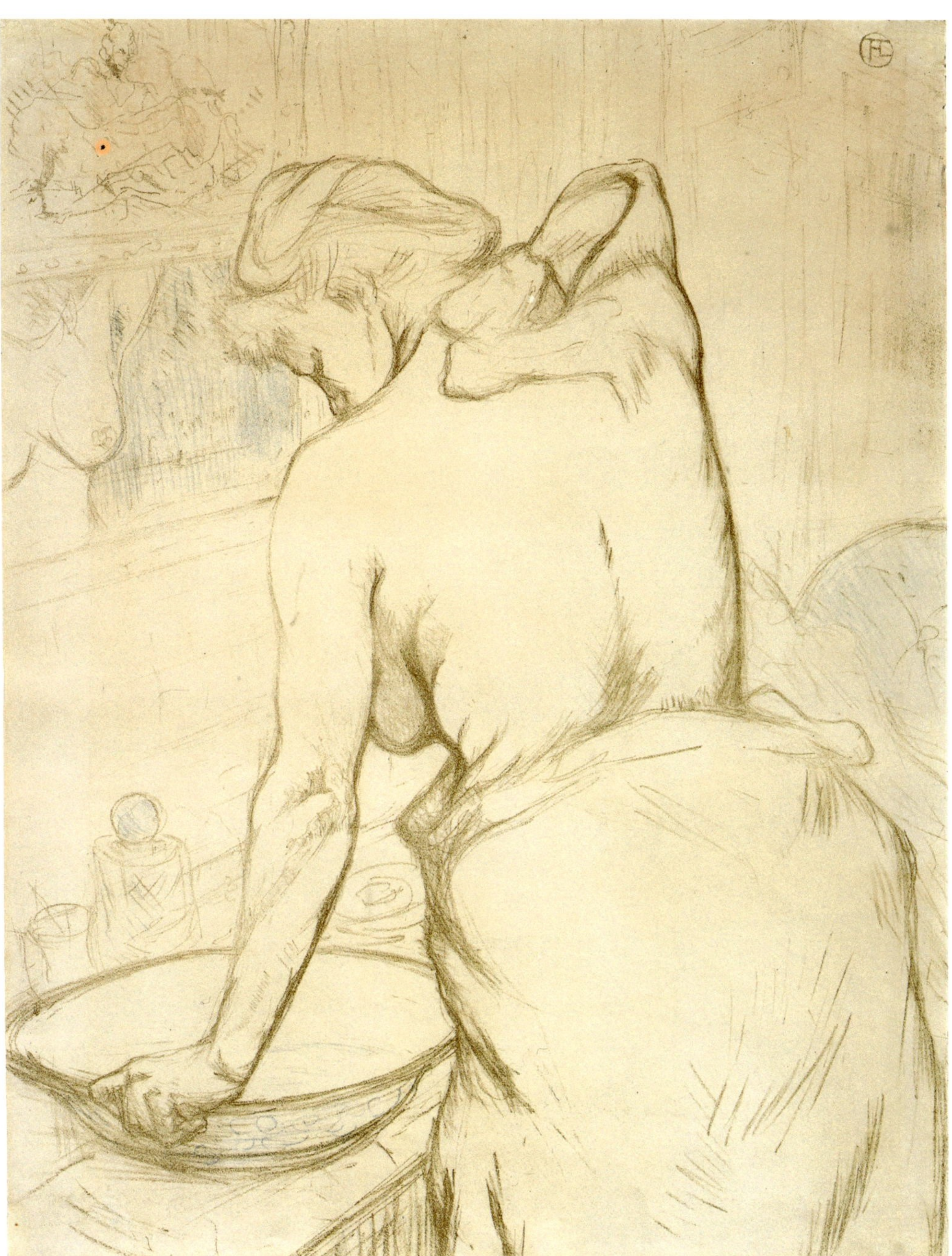

PLATE 52
Henri de Toulouse-Lautrec, *Woman at Her Toilette, Washing Herself*, from the album *Elles*, 1896, color lithograph

Woman at Her Toilette, Washing Herself highlights the artist's superb draftsmanship. Henri de Toulouse-Lautrec captured the curve of the model's back, the wispy fringe of her bangs, and the solidity of her washbasin using a variety of strokes of the lithographic crayon. **MWC**

PLATE 53
Henri de Toulouse-Lautrec, *Woman at the Tub*,
from the album *Elles*, 1896, color lithograph

Henri de Toulouse-Lautrec's depictions of
brothels are not without humor. In this scene,
the shallow tub with its floating sponge suggests
a giant fried egg in a skillet. Above the bent figure hangs a partial image of a nude woman
accompanied by a goose that appears ready to
peck her bare bottom. **MWC**

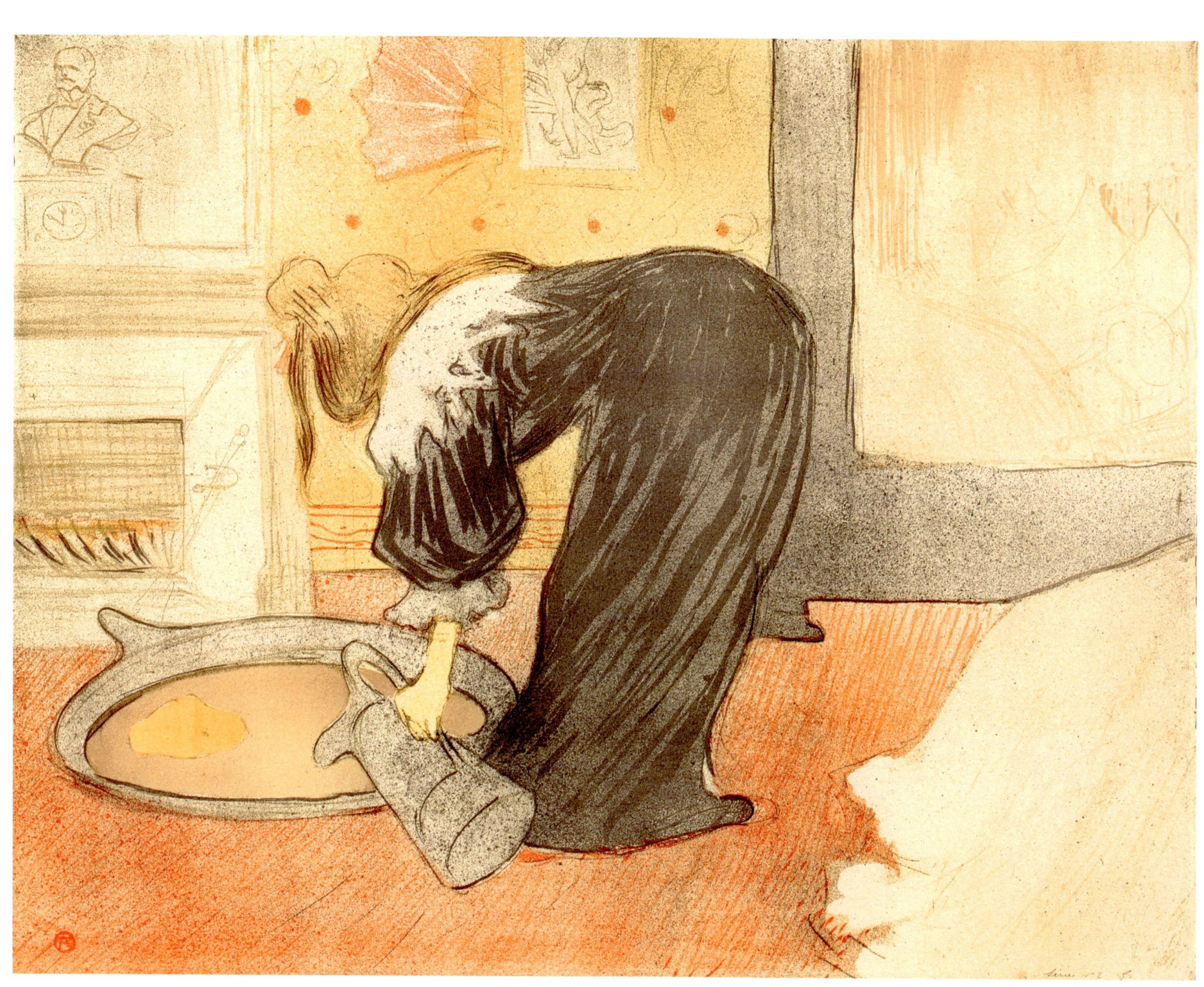

PLATE 54
Henri de Toulouse-Lautrec, *Queen of Joy*, 1892,
color lithograph

Queen of Joy: Customs of the Demi-Monde was a
thinly veiled (and antisemitic) novel likely based
on the life of Baron Rothschild. A contemporary
critic hailed Henri de Toulouse-Lautrec's poster
as "bright, attractive and superbly perverse." **MWC**

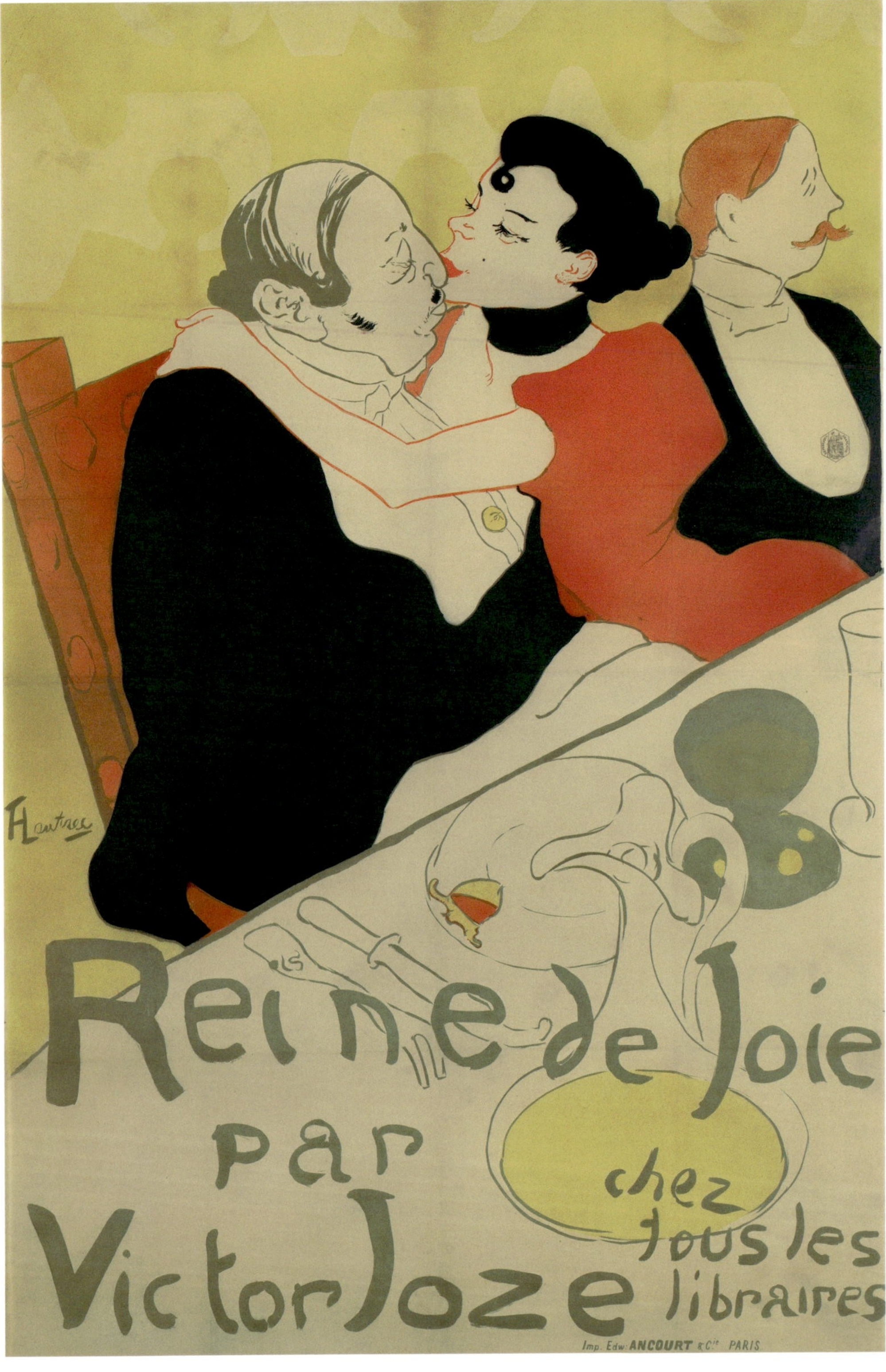

PLATE 55
Henri de Toulouse-Lautrec, *Debauchery*, cover
for *Catalogue d'Affiches artistiques*, 1896, color
lithograph

Henri de Toulouse-Lautrec's images of deca-
dent behavior sometimes feature humorous elements. Here, the exaggerated poses of the figures,
the lecherous expression on the man's face, and
the woman's upturned nose and precarious glass
of champagne suggest equal parts farce and lust.
MWC

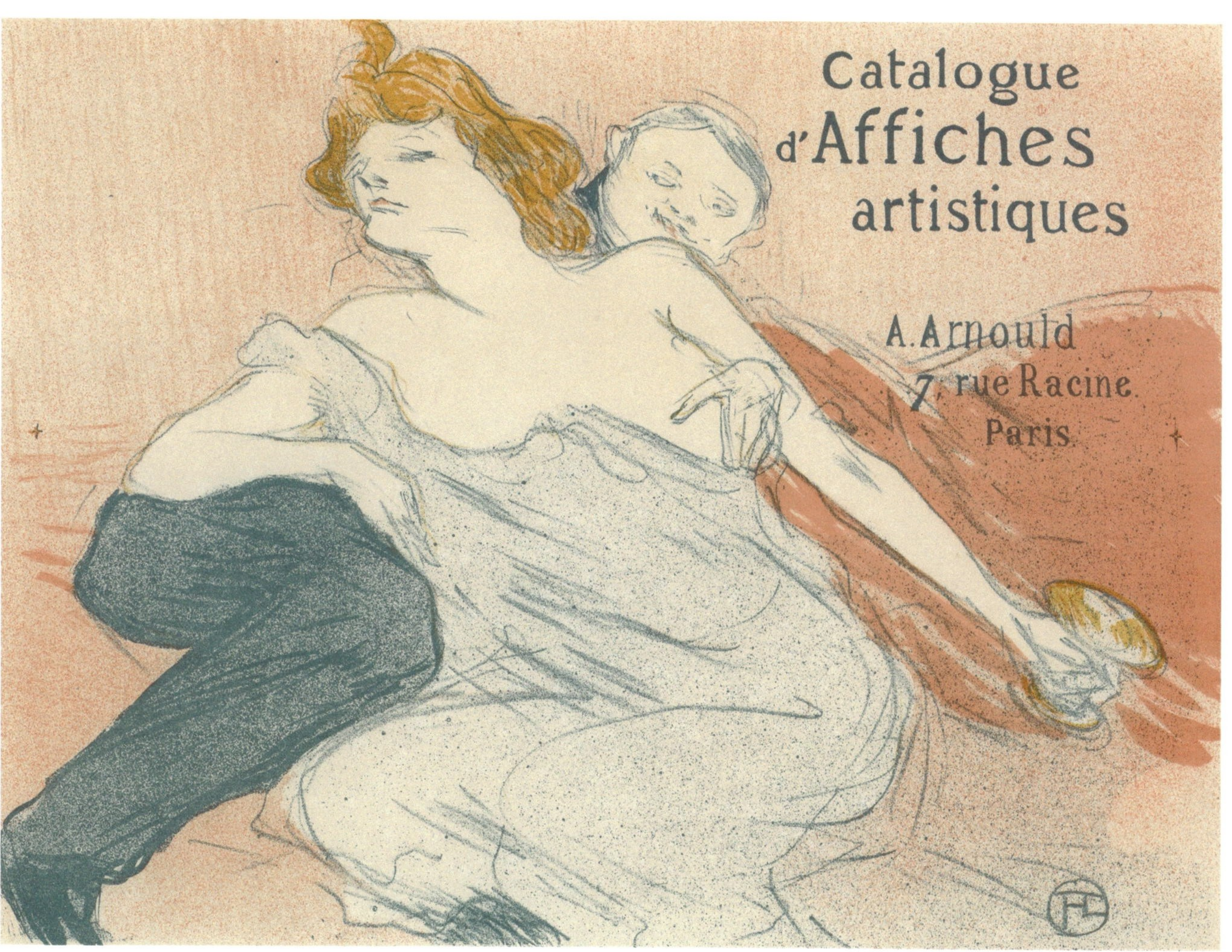

Catalogue
d'Affiches
artistiques

A. Arnould
7, rue Racine.
Paris

PLATE 56
Henri de Toulouse-Lautrec, *The Seated Clowness*,
from the album *Elles*, 1896, color lithograph

Unlike the other sheets in the *Elles* series, all of
which take place in a brothel, this dazzling lithograph depicts the acrobat and dancer known as
Cha-U-Kao (a play on words that references the
chaos of the cancan) in another setting, perhaps a
masked ball, judging from the figures behind her.
MWC

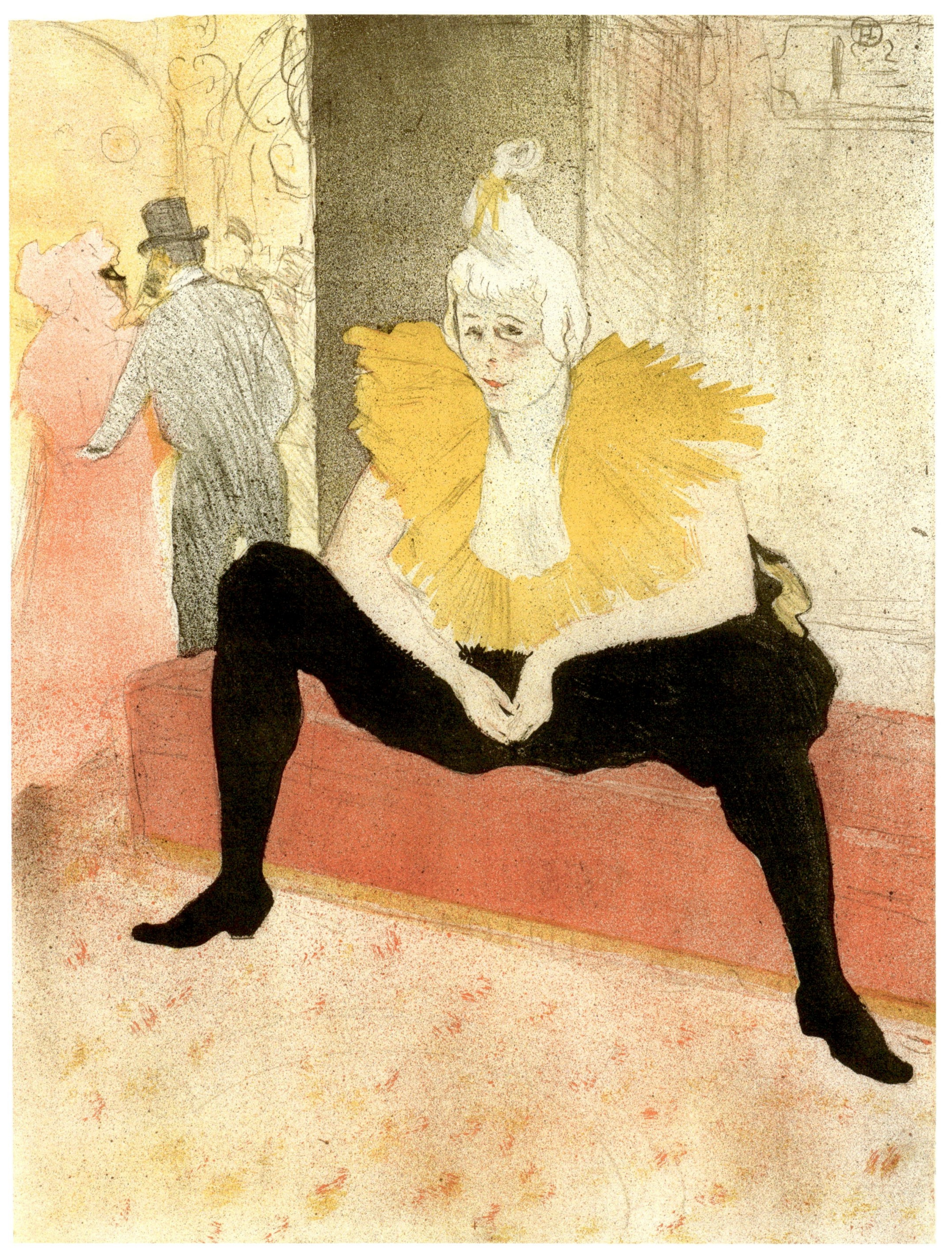

Exhibition Checklist

The artworks are listed according to their arrangement in the galleries.

Introduction
Floating World in Edo and Bohemian Paris

Miyagawa school
Picnicking under Cherry Blossoms and Boating on the Sumida River, mid-1700s
Pair of six-panel screens; ink, color, and gold on paper
Each screen: 36⅜ × 107½ in. (92.4 × 273.1 cm)
Seattle Art Museum, Margaret E. Fuller Purchase Fund, 62.133.1–2
Plate 1

Jules Chéret
Ball at the Moulin Rouge, 1889
Color lithograph
48¾ × 34¾ in. (123.8 × 88.3 cm)
Collection of John and Joyce Price
Plate 3

Anonymous
Ombres Parisiennes, ca. 1905
Color lithograph
32¼ × 46½ in. (81.9 × 118.1 cm)
Promised Gift to the Portland Art Museum from Daniel Bergsvik and Donald Hastler

Henri de Toulouse-Lautrec
Divan Japonais, 1892
Color lithograph
31½ × 23½ in. (80 × 59.7 cm)
Collection of Mary and Allan Kollar
Plate 6

Henri Rivière
Thirty-Six Views of the Eiffel Tower, 1902
Album of 36 color lithographs
Album: 11½ × 9¼ × ⅝ in. (11.5 × 29.2 cm)
Image: 10½ × 9 in. (26.7 × 22.9 cm)
Portland Art Museum, Museum Purchase: Jean Y. Roth Memorial Fund, 2012.104.1a–b
Plate 4

Katsushika Hokusai
Yoshida on the Tōkaidō, from the series *Thirty-Six Views of Mount Fuji*, ca. 1830–32
Woodblock print; ink and color on paper
10 × 14¾ in. (25.4 × 37.5 cm)
Seattle Art Museum, Gift of Mary and Allan Kollar, in honor of the 75th Anniversary of the Seattle Art Museum, 2010.47.1
Plate 2

Jules Chéret
Exhibition of Japanese Prints, 1890
Color lithograph
32⅛ × 46⅝ in. (96.5 × 134 cm)
Collection of John and Joyce Price
Plate 5

Entertainment
Shitamachi and Montmartre

Henri de Toulouse-Lautrec
Moulin Rouge: La Goulue, 1891
Color lithograph
74¹³⁄₁₆ × 45⅞ in. (190 × 116.6 cm)
Spencer M. Hawes
Plate 13

Théophile Alexandre Steinlen
Tour of the Chat Noir, 1896
Color lithograph
53⅞ × 38⅝ in. (136.8 × 98.1 cm)
Collection of John and Joyce Price
Plate 14

Jacques Villon
Dancer at the Moulin Rouge, 1899
Color lithograph
11¼ × 8⅜ in. (28.6 × 21.3 cm)
Portland Art Museum, Gift of James D. Burke in honor of Walker Cahall, 2015.75.3

Henri de Toulouse-Lautrec
The Englishman at the Moulin Rouge, 1892
Color lithograph
18¼ × 14¾ in. (46.4 × 37.5 cm)
Collection of Mary and Allan Kollar
Plate 15

Félix Vallotton
Ah! La Pé . . . La Pé . . . La Pépinière!!! Revue, 1898
Color lithograph
48 × 35¾ in. (121.9 × 90.8 cm)
Collection of John and Joyce Price
Plate 16

Henri de Toulouse-Lautrec
Program cover for the play *L'Argent* (Money), 1895
Color lithograph
12½ × 15½ in. (31.8 × 24.1 cm)
Collection of John and Joyce Price
Plate 17

Henri de Toulouse-Lautrec
Playbill for *Le Chariot de Terre Cuite* (The Little Clay Cart), 1895
Color lithograph
17⅜ × 10⅞ in. (44.1 × 27.6 cm)
Collection of John and Joyce Price

Henri de Toulouse-Lautrec
Le Gage, 1897
Lithograph
11⁷⁄₁₆ × 9¹¹⁄₁₆ in. (29 × 24.6 cm)
Collection of John and Joyce Price

Henri de Toulouse-Lautrec
A Scene from Offenbach's La Belle Hélène, 1900
Lithograph
27¹⁵⁄₁₆ × 20⁷⁄₁₆ in. (71 × 51.9 cm)
Collection of John and Joyce Price

Jules Chéret
La Farandole, 1884
Lithograph
28 × 21¾ in. (71.1 × 55.2 cm)
Collection of John and Joyce Price

Théophile Alexandre Steinlen
La Rêve, 1890
Color lithograph
23⅞ × 31⅜ in. (60.6 × 79.7 cm)
Promised Gift to the Portland Art Museum
from Daniel Bergsvik and Donald Hastler

Suzuki Harunobu
A Dancer Performing Heron Maiden, ca. 1766–68
Woodblock print; ink and color on paper
8⅞ × 12¾ in. (22.5 × 32.4 cm)
Seattle Art Museum, Gift of Mary and Allan
Kollar, in honor of the 75th Anniversary of the
Seattle Art Museum, 2013.31.3
Plate 9

Kitagawa Utamaro
Hands inside the Sleeves, from the series *Eight Views
of Tea Stalls in Celebrated Places*, ca. 1795–96
Woodblock print; ink and color on paper
15 × 9½ in. (38.1 × 24.1 cm)
Seattle Art Museum, Gift of Mary and Allan
Kollar, in honor of the 75th Anniversary of the
Seattle Art Museum, 2017.23.6

Utagawa Hiroshige
Moon Cape, from the series *One Hundred Views of
Famous Places in Edo*, 1857
Woodblock print; ink and color on paper
14⅛ × 9¾ in. (35.9 × 24.8 cm)
Seattle Art Museum, Gift of Mary and Allan
Kollar, in honor of the 75th Anniversary of the
Seattle Art Museum, 2017.23.23
Plate 11

Utagawa Kunisada
Confronting the Cherry Spirit, 1834
Woodblock print; ink and color on paper
20¾ × 41 in. (52.7 × 104.2 cm)
Seattle Art Museum, Gift of Mr. and
Mrs. Hamilton R. Harris, 85.220
Plate 7

Kitagawa Utamaro
Act Four, from the series *Treasury of the Forty-Seven
Loyal Retainers*, 1801–2
Woodblock print; ink and color on paper
15¼ × 10½ in. (38.7 × 26.7 cm)
Seattle Art Museum, Gift of Mary and Allan
Kollar, in honor of the 75th Anniversary of the
Seattle Art Museum, 2017.23.14

Kitagawa Utamaro
Act Six, from the series *Treasury of the Forty-Seven
Loyal Retainers*, 1801–2
Woodblock print; ink and color on paper
15 × 10 in. (38.1 × 25.4 cm)
Seattle Art Museum, Gift of Mary and Allan
Kollar, in honor of the 75th Anniversary of the
Seattle Art Museum, 2017.23.15

Utagawa Kunisada
Actors in an Offstage Scene, ca. 1850
Woodblock print; ink and color on paper
14¼ × 9⅞ in. (36.2 × 25.1 cm)
Seattle Art Museum, Gift of Capt. D. W.
Carpenter, 53.136
Plate 8

Utagawa Yoshitora
Fashionable Spring Moon, ca. 1847–52
Woodblock print; ink and color on paper
14⅜ × 10 in. (36.5 × 25.4 cm)
Seattle Art Museum, Gift of Capt. D. W.
Carpenter, 53.140
Plate 12

Kitagawa Utamaro
Teahouse Waitress behind a Bamboo Blind, from the
series *Eight Views of Tea Stalls in Celebrated Places*,
ca. 1795–96
Woodblock print; ink and color on paper
15⅜ × 10¼ in. (39.1 × 26 cm)
Seattle Art Museum, Gift of Mary and Allan
Kollar, in honor of the 75th Anniversary of the
Seattle Art Museum, 2017.23.8
Plate 10

Kitagawa Utamaro
*Okita of the Naniwaya Studying Her Face in a Hand
Mirror*, 1795–96
Woodblock print; ink and color on paper
14½ × 9½ in. (36.8 × 24.1 cm)
Seattle Art Museum, Gift of Mary and Allan
Kollar, in honor of the 75th Anniversary of the
Seattle Art Museum, 2017.23.7

Celebrity Culture

Henri de Toulouse-Lautrec
Yvette Guilbert Onstage, cover for the album *Yvette
Guilbert*, 1898
Lithograph
20³⁄₁₆ × 14¾ in. (51.3 × 37.5 cm)
Collection of John and Joyce Price
Plate 27

Henri de Toulouse-Lautrec
Yvette Guilbert before the Prompter's Box, 1898
Lithograph
19¾ × 14¾ in. (50.2 × 37.5 cm)
Collection of John and Joyce Price

Henri de Toulouse-Lautrec
Yvette Guilbert Bowing, from the album *Yvette
Guilbert*, 1898
Lithograph
12¾ × 10½ in. (32.4 × 26.7 cm)
Collection of John and Joyce Price
Plate 28

Henri Gabriel Ibels
Yvette Guilbert, 1894
Lithograph
24 × 18¾ in. (82.6 × 47.6 cm)
Collection of John and Joyce Price

Ferdinand-Sigismund Bac
Yvette Guilbert—Scala, 1893
Color lithograph
13⅝ × 11⅜ in. (34.6 × 28.9 cm)
Collection of John and Joyce Price

Charles Reutlinger
Yvette Guilbert, 1894
Gelatin silver print
6½ × 4¼ in. (16.5 × 10.8 cm)
Collection of John and Joyce Price

Yvette Guilbert
Gelatin silver print
5⅜ × 3⅜ in. (13.7 × 8.6 cm)
Collection of John and Joyce Price

Henri de Toulouse-Lautrec
At the Moulin Rouge: La Goulue and Her Sister, 1892
Color lithograph
18⅛ × 13⅝ in. (46 × 34.6 cm)
Collection of John and Joyce Price
Plate 29

Henri de Toulouse-Lautrec
La Goulue, 1894
Lithograph
13½ × 10½ in. (34.3 × 26.7 cm)
Collection of John and Joyce Price

Henri de Toulouse-Lautrec
Jane Avril, 1893
Color lithograph
50¾ × 36½ in. (128.9 × 92.7 cm)
Spencer M. Hawes
Plate 30

Henri de Toulouse-Lautrec
Troupe de Mademoiselle Eglantine (Mademoiselle
Eglantine's Troupe), 1896
Color lithograph
23¾ × 31⅜ in. (60.3 × 79.7 cm)
Collection of John and Joyce Price
Plate 31

Henri de Toulouse-Lautrec
May Belfort, 1895
Color lithograph
31 × 23¾ in. (78.7 × 60.3 cm)
Collection of John and Joyce Price
Plate 32

Henri de Toulouse-Lautrec
May Milton, 1895
Color lithograph
30¾ × 22⅞ in. (78.1 × 58.1 cm)
Collection of John and Joyce Price
Plate 33

Jules Chéret
Loïe Fuller, 1893
Color lithograph
47⅞ × 33⅝ in. (121.6 × 85.4 cm)
Collection of John and Joyce Price
Plate 34

Emmanuel-Joseph-Raphael Orazi
Loïe Fuller Theatre, 1900
Color lithograph
78¼ × 25¼ in. (198.8 × 64.1 cm)
Promised Gift to the Portland Art Museum
from Daniel Bergsvik and Donald Hastler

Henri de Toulouse-Lautrec
Aristide Bruant in His Cabaret, 1893
Color lithograph
52¾ × 38 in. (134 × 96.5 cm)
Collection of John and Joyce Price
Plate 35

Henri de Toulouse-Lautrec
Aristide Bruant at the Mirliton, 1893
Lithograph
31⁹⁄₁₆ × 22⅜ in. (80.2 × 56.8 cm)
Collection of John and Joyce Price
Plate 36

Henri de Toulouse-Lautrec
Marcelle Lender, 1895
Color lithograph
22¾ × 16½ in. (57.8 × 41.9 cm)
Spencer M. Hawes
Plate 37

Henri de Toulouse-Lautrec
Pour Toi, 1893
Lithograph
11⅝ × 8½ in. (29.5 × 21.6 cm)
Collection of John and Joyce Price

Henri de Toulouse-Lautrec
Cléo de Mérode, 1898
Lithograph
12½ × 10½ in. (31.8 × 26.7 cm)
Collection of John and Joyce Price

Tōshūsai Sharaku
The Actor Sawamura Sōjūrō III as Kujaku Saburō, 1794
Woodblock print; ink and color on paper
12¾ × 8¾ in. (32.4 × 22.2 cm)
Seattle Art Museum, Gift of Mary and Allan
Kollar, in honor of the 75th Anniversary of the
Seattle Art Museum, 2013.31.10
Plate 18

Utagawa Kunihisa
The Actor Segawa Michinosuke in a Female Role, 1804
Woodblock print; ink and color on paper
14½ × 10 in. (36.8 × 25.4 cm)
Seattle Art Museum, Gift of Mary and Allan
Kollar, in honor of the 75th Anniversary of the
Seattle Art Museum, 2014.32.7
Plate 19

Ippitsusai Bunchō
*The Actor Onoe Matsutake I in the Role of a Young
Woman of Fashion*, 1780s
Woodblock print; ink and color on paper
11⅞ × 5⅝ in. (30.2 × 14.3 cm)
Seattle Art Museum, Gift of Mary and Allan
Kollar, in honor of the 75th Anniversary of the
Seattle Art Museum, 2013.31.9

Katsukawa Shunshō
*The Actor Ichikawa Danjūrō V as the Spirit of Monk
Seigen*, 1772
Woodblock print; ink and color with metallic
pigments on paper
12¼ × 5⅝ in. (31.1 × 14.3 cm)
Seattle Art Museum, Asian Art Acquisition Fund,
2013.10.2
Plate 20

Katsukawa Shunei
The Actor Ichikawa Danjūrō V, 1780s
Woodblock print; ink and color on paper
12⅞ × 6 in. (32.7 × 15.2 cm)
Seattle Art Museum, Gift of Mr. and
Mrs. Hamilton R. Harris, 85.361
Plate 21

Torii Kiyomitsu
*The Actor Ōtani Hiroji II as Kazusa no Shichirō
Kagekiyo*, ca. 1750
Woodblock print; ink and color on paper
12 × 5⅝ in. (30.5 × 14.3 cm)
Seattle Art Museum, Gift of Mary and Allan
Kollar, 2011.40.7
Plate 22

Katsukawa Shunkō
*The Actor Nakamura Nakazō I in the Role of
a Daimyo's Retainer*, 1780–85
Woodblock print; ink and color on paper
12¼ × 6 in. (31.1 × 15.2 cm)
Seattle Art Museum, Gift of Mary and Allan
Kollar, in honor of the 75th Anniversary of the
Seattle Art Museum, 2013.31.8

Katsukawa Shunshō
The Actor Ichikawa Danjūrō V as Arakawa Tarō, 1778
Woodblock print; ink and color on paper
12½ × 5¾ in. (31.8 × 14.6 cm)
Collection of Mary and Allan Kollar
Plate 23

Katsukawa Shunkō
The Actor Nakamura Tomijūrō in the Lion Dance, 1778
Woodblock print; ink and color on paper
17⅘ × 6 in. (45.2 × 15.2 cm)
Collection of Mary and Allan Kollar
Plate 24

Kitagawa Utamaro
Portrait of Osan, ca. 1800
Woodblock print; ink and color on paper
15 × 9¾ in. (38 × 24.8 cm)
Collection of Mary and Allan Kollar
Plate 25

Kitagawa Utamaro
Pensive Love, ca. 1793
Woodblock print; ink and color on paper with
pink mica
15 × 10 in. (38.1 × 25.4 cm)
Private Collection, New York
Plate 26

Pleasure Quarters

Utagawa Hiroshige
Dawn at the Entrance to Yoshiwara, from the series
One Hundred Views of Famous Places in Edo, 1857
Woodblock print; ink and color on paper
13½ × 9 in. (34.3 × 22.9 cm)
Collection of Mary and Allan Kollar
Plate 38

Kitagawa Utamaro
Shizuka of the Tamaya House, from the series *A Complete Set of the Great Beauties of the Present Day*, 1794
Woodblock print; ink and color on paper
15 × 9¾ in. (38.1 × 24.8 cm)
Seattle Art Museum, Gift of Mary and Allan
Kollar, in honor of the 75th Anniversary of the
Seattle Art Museum, 2017.23.4
Plate 39

Utagawa Toyokuni
Yosooi of the Matsubaya House, 1798–1800
Woodblock print; ink and color on paper
14⅞ × 11¼ in. (37.8 × 28.6 cm)
Seattle Art Museum, Gift of Mary and Allan
Kollar, in honor of the 75th Anniversary of the
Seattle Art Museum, 2014.32.5

Hosoda Eisui
Kisegawa of the Matsubaya House Holding a Fan, 1800
Woodblock print; ink and color on paper
14½ × 9¾ in. (36.8 × 24.8 cm)
Seattle Art Museum, Gift of Mary and Allan
Kollar, in honor of the 75th Anniversary of the
Seattle Art Museum, 2014.32.2

Isoda Koryūsai
Sugawara of the Tsuruya House with Two Attendants,
from the series *Models for Fashion*, ca. 1775
Woodblock print; ink and color on paper
14⅞ × 10 in. (37.8 × 25.4 cm)
Seattle Art Museum, Gift of Mary and Allan
Kollar, in honor of the 75th Anniversary of the
Seattle Art Museum, 2013.31.6
Plate 42

Kitagawa Utamaro
Delivering a Letter, from the series *Elegant Five-
Needled Pine*, 1797–98
Woodblock print; ink and color on paper
13¼ × 10 in. (33.5 × 25.4 cm)
Collection of Mary and Allan Kollar
Plate 40

Torii Kiyomine
A Beauty of the Eastern Brocade, ca. 1804–10
Woodblock print; ink and color on paper
15 × 10 in. (38.1 × 25.4 cm)
Collection of Mary and Allan Kollar
Plate 43

Hosoda Eisui
Segawa of the Matsubaya House, 1800
Woodblock print; ink and color on paper
15 × 10 in. (38.1 × 25.4 cm)
Seattle Art Museum, Gift of Mary and Allan
Kollar, in honor of the 75th Anniversary of the
Seattle Art Museum, 2014.32.3

Kitagawa Utamaro
Beauty Reading a Letter under a Mosquito Net, 1795–98
Woodblock print; ink and color on paper
15 × 10 in. (38.1 × 25.4 cm)
Seattle Art Museum, Gift of Mary and Allan
Kollar, in honor of the 75th Anniversary of the
Seattle Art Museum, 2017.23.9

Kitagawa Utamaro
Tagasode of the Tamaya House, 1800–1802
Woodblock print; ink and color on paper
15½ × 10½ in. (39.4 × 26.7 cm)
Seattle Art Museum, Gift of Mary and Allan
Kollar, in honor of the 75th Anniversary of the
Seattle Art Museum, 2017.23.13
Plate 41

Utagawa Toyokuni
The Much-Frequented Komachi (Kayoi Komachi),
ca. 1795
Woodblock print; ink and color on paper
14⅝ × 10 in. (37.2 × 25.6 cm)
Private Collection, New York
Plate 44

Henri de Toulouse-Lautrec
"Pauvre Pierreuse!," 1893
Color lithograph
12⅛ × 9 in. (30.8 × 22.9 cm)
Collection of John and Joyce Price

Henri de Toulouse-Lautrec
Étude de Femme, 1893
Color lithograph
10½ × 6⅞ in. (26.7 × 17.5 cm)
Collection of John and Joyce Price

Henri de Toulouse-Lautrec
Program for Le Theatre Libre, 1893
Color lithograph
7¾ × 6⅛ in. (63.5 × 48.3 cm)
Collection of John and Joyce Price

Henri de Toulouse-Lautrec
Cover for the album *Elles*, 1896
Color lithograph
25 × 19 in. (63.5 × 48.3 cm)
Collection of John and Joyce Price
Plate 49

Henri de Toulouse-Lautrec
Woman in a Corset, from the album *Elles*, 1896
Color lithograph
20⅝ × 15⅞ in. (52.4 × 40.3 cm)
Portland Art Museum, Gift from the Collection of
Laura and Roger Meier, 2003.10.6
Plate 50

Henri de Toulouse-Lautrec
Woman with Hand Mirror, from the album *Elles*, 1896
Color lithograph
20½ × 15¾ in. (52.1 × 40 cm)
Portland Art Museum, Gift from the Collection of
Laura and Roger Meier, 2003.10.3
Plate 51

Henri de Toulouse-Lautrec
Woman at Her Toilette, Washing Herself, from the
album *Elles*, 1896
Color lithograph
20½ × 15⅞ in. (52.1 × 40.3 cm)
Portland Art Museum, Gift from the Collection of
Laura and Roger Meier, 2003.10.2
Plate 52

Henri de Toulouse-Lautrec
Woman at the Tub, from the album *Elles*, 1896
Color lithograph
19¾ × 20¾ in. (50.2 × 52.7 cm)
Portland Art Museum, Gift from the Collection of
Laura and Roger Meier, 2003.10.3
Plate 53

Henri de Toulouse-Lautrec
Queen of Joy, 1892
Color lithograph
53¾ × 36⅜ in. (136.5 × 92.4 cm)
Collection of John and Joyce Price
Plate 54

Henri de Toulouse-Lautrec
Debauchery, cover for *Catalogue d'Affiches artistiques*,
1896
Color lithograph
9¼ × 12½ in. (23.5 × 31.8 cm)
Collection of John and Joyce Price
Plate 55

Henri de Toulouse-Lautrec
Old Flirts, 1895
Lithograph
10⅞ × 8⅛ in. (27.6 × 20.6 cm)
Collection of John and Joyce Price

Henri de Toulouse-Lautrec
The Seated Clowness, from the album *Elles*, 1896
Color lithograph
20 × 15¾ in. (50.8 × 40 cm)
Collection of Mary and Allan Kollar
Plate 56

Keisen Eishi
A Geisha Wards off Unwanted Attention, ca. 1795
Woodblock print; ink on paper
25½ × 4¾ in. (64.8 × 12.1 cm)
Collection of Mary and Allan Kollar
Plate 45

Torii Kiyonobu I
A Young Girl with Her Client, ca. 1710s
Woodblock print; ink on paper
10¼ × 14⁹⁄₁₆ in. (26 × 37 cm)
Seattle Art Museum, Gift of Mary and Allan
Kollar, 2011.40.1
Plate 46

Torii Kiyonobu I
A Sex Worker and Client Watched by Her Attendant,
ca. 1710
Woodblock print; ink on paper
10⅛ × 15 in. (25.7 × 38.1 cm)
Seattle Art Museum, Gift of Mary and Allan
Kollar, 2011.40.2

Kitagawa Utamaro
A High-Ranking Yūjo with a Client, 1799
Woodblock print; ink and color on paper
10 × 15⅛ in. (25.4 × 38.4 cm)
Seattle Art Museum, Gift of Mary and Allan
Kollar, in honor of the 75th Anniversary of the
Seattle Art Museum, 2017.23.12
Plate 47

Kitagawa Utamaro
Needlework, from the *Untitled Series of Scenes of
Everyday Life*, ca. 1797–98
Woodblock print; ink and color on paper
15⅓ × 10⅓ in. (38.8 × 26.2 cm)
Private Collection, New York
Plate 48

Kitagawa Utamaro
"Gun" Prostitute, from the series *Five Shades of Ink
in the Northern Quarter*, 1794–95
Woodblock print; ink and color on paper
14¾ × 10⅛ in. (37.5 × 25.6 cm)
Private Collection, New York

Further Readings

Asano, Shūgō, and Timothy Clark. *The Passionate Art of Kitagawa Utamaro*. Exh. cat. London: British Museum Press, 1995.

Breuer, Karin. *Japanesque: The Japanese Print in the Era of Impressionism*. Exh. cat. London: Prestel, 2010.

Brocklehurst, Hannah, and Frances Fowle. *Pin-Ups: Toulouse-Lautrec and the Art of Celebrity*. Exh. cat. Edinburgh: National Galleries of Scotland, 2018.

Burnham, Helen, Mary Weaver Chapin, and Joanna Wendel. *Toulouse-Lautrec and the Stars of Paris*. Exh. cat. Boston: MFA Publications; Museum of Fine Arts, 2019.

Burnham, Helen, Sarah Thompson, and Jane Braun. *Looking East: Western Artists and the Allure of Japan*. Exh. cat. Boston: MFA Publications; Museum of Fine Arts, 2014.

Castleman, Riva, and Wolfgang Wittrock, eds. *Henri de Toulouse-Lautrec: Images of the 1890s*. Exh. cat. New York: Museum of Modern Art, 1985.

Cate, Phillip Dennis, Gale B. Murray, and Richard Thompson. *Prints Abound: Paris in the 1890s; From the Collections of Virginia and Ira Jackson and the National Gallery of Art*. Exh. cat. Washington, DC: National Gallery of Art; London: Lund Humphries, 2000.

Chapin, Mary Weaver. *Posters of Paris: Toulouse-Lautrec and His Contemporaries*. Exh. cat. London: Prestel, 2012.

Chisaburō, Yamada, and Tatsuji Ohmori, eds. *Japonisme in Art: An International Symposium*. Tokyo: Committee for the Year; Kodansha International, 2001.

Clark, Timothy, Donald Jenkins, and Osamu Ueda. *The Actor's Image: Printmakers of the Katsukawa School*. Chicago: Art Institute of Chicago; Princeton, NJ: Princeton University Press, 1994.

D'Avenel, Georges. *Le Mécanisme de la vie moderne*. Paris: Librairie Armand Colin, 1902.

Davis, Julie Nelson. *Partners in Print: Artistic Collaboration and the Ukiyo-e Market*. Honolulu: University of Hawai'i Press, 2014.

——. *Picturing the Floating World: Ukiyo-e in Context*. Honolulu: University of Hawai'i Press, 2021.

——. *Utamaro and the Spectacle of Beauty*. London: Reaktion Books, 2007.

Foxwell, Chelsea, and Anne Leonard. *Awash in Color: French and Japanese Prints*. Exh. cat. Chicago: Smart Museum of Art; University of Chicago Press, 2012.

Guth, Christine. *Art of Edo Japan: The Artist and the City, 1615–1868*. New York: Harry N. Abrams, 1996.

Hickman, Money L. "Views of the Floating World." *MFA Bulletin* 76 (1978): 4–33. http://www.jstor.org/stable/4171617.

Ives, Colta Feller. *The Great Wave: The Influence of Japanese Woodcuts on French Prints*. Exh. cat. New York: Metropolitan Museum of Art, 1974.

——. *Toulouse-Lautrec in the Metropolitan Museum of Art*. Exh. cat. New York: Metropolitan Museum of Art, 1996.

McClain, James L., John M. Merriman, and Ugawa Kaoru, eds. *Edo and Paris: Urban Life and the State in the Early Modern Era*. Ithaca, NY: Cornell University Press, 1997.

Meech, Julia, Jane Oliver, and John T. Carpenter, eds. *Designed for Pleasure: The World of Edo Japan in Prints and Paintings, 1680–1860*. Exh. cat. New York: Asia Society; Seattle: Japanese Art Society of America, 2008.

Morse, Anne Nishimura, ed. *Drama and Desire: Japanese Paintings from the Floating World, 1690–1850*. Exh. cat. Boston: Museum of Fine Arts, 2007.

Narazaki, Muneshige. *Exposition Toulouse-Lautrec et Utamaro*. Exh. cat. Tokyo: Mainichi Shimbun Sha, 1980.

Roche, Catherine Cawood. *Fleeting Beauty: Japanese Woodblock Prints*. Exh. cat. Seattle: Seattle Art Museum, 2010.

Screech, Timon. *Sex and the Floating World: Erotic Images in Japan, 1700–1820*. Honolulu: University of Hawai'i Press, 1999.

——. *Tokyo Before Tokyo: Power and Magic in the Shogun's City of Edo*. London: Reaktion Books, 2020.

Suzuki, Sarah. *The Paris of Toulouse-Lautrec: Prints and Posters from the Museum of Modern Art*. New York: Museum of Modern Art, 2014.

Thomson, Richard, Phillip Dennis Cate, and Mary Weaver Chapin. *Toulouse-Lautrec and Montmartre*. Exh. cat. Washington, DC: National Gallery of Art, 2005.

This book is published in conjunction with the exhibition *Renegade Edo and Paris: Japanese Prints and Toulouse-Lautrec*, presented at the Seattle Art Museum from July 21 to December 3, 2023.

Lead Sponsors

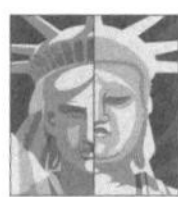

Tateuchi Foundation

Allan and Mary Kollar

Generous Support
Katherine Agen Baillargeon Endowment
Blakemore Foundation
Mary Ann and Henry James Asian Art Exhibition
    Endowment

Library of Congress Control Number: 2022951114
ISBN 978-0-932216-07-6

Published by Seattle Art Museum
www.seattleartmuseum.org

Distributed by University of Washington Press
www.uwapress.uw.edu

Produced by Marquand Books, Seattle
www.marquandbooks.com

Edited by Sheri Walter
Designed by Ryan Polich
Typeset in Wolpe Pegasus, Min Sans, and
    Founders Grotesk by Maggie Lee
Proofread by Bruno George
Color management by I/O Color, Seattle
Printed and bound in China by Artron Art Group

Cover (clockwise from top left): Utagawa Hiroshige, *Dawn at the Entrance to Yoshiwara* (detail), from the series *One Hundred Views of Famous Places in Edo*, 1857, woodblock print; Kitagawa Utamaro, *Shizuka of the Tamaya House* (detail), from the series *A Complete Set of the Great Beauties of the Present Day*, 1794, woodblock print; Henri de Toulouse-Lautrec, *Jane Avril* (detail), 1893, color lithograph

Page 2 (top to bottom): Henri de Toulouse-Lautrec, *The Englishman at the Moulin Rouge* (detail), 1892, color lithograph; Kitagawa Utamaro, *Delivering a Letter* (detail), from the series *Elegant Five-Needled Pine*, 1797–98, woodblock print

Page 3 (left to right): Katsukawa Shunkō, *The Actor Nakamura Tomijūrō in the Lion Dance* (detail), 1778, woodblock print; Henri de Toulouse-Lautrec, *Divan Japonais* (detail), 1892, color lithograph

Page 12: Kitagawa Utamaro, *Pensive Love* (detail), ca. 1793, woodblock print

Page 20: Henri de Toulouse-Lautrec, *Troupe de Mademoiselle Eglantine* (Mademoiselle Eglantine's Troupe) (detail), 1896, color lithograph